# MIND GYM

## AN ATHLETE'S GUIDE TO
## INNER EXCELLENCE

### GARY MACK WITH DAVID CASSTEVENS
#### FOREWORD BY ALEX RODRIGUEZ

## *Contemporary Books*

Chicago   New York   San Francisco   Lisbon   London   Madrid   Mexico City
Milan   New Delhi   San Juan   Seoul   Singapore   Sydney   Toronto

**Library of Congress Cataloging-in-Publication Data**

Mack, Gary.
    Mind gym : an athlete's guide to inner excellence / Gary Mack with David Casstevens ;
foreword by Alex Rodriguez
        p.    cm.
    ISBN 0-8092-9674-8 (hardcover)    0-07-139597-0 (paperback)
    1. Sports—Psychological aspects.    2. Success—Psychological aspects.
I. Casstevens, David.    II. Title.

GV706.4 .M32    2001
796'.01—dc21                                                                    00-64387

*This book is dedicated to all the athletes, coaches, and teams
we have had the privilege of working with.*

# Contemporary Books

### A Division of The McGraw·Hill Companies

        8 9 0    LBM/LBM    0 9 8 7 6 5

ISBN 0-8092-9674-8 (hardcover)
        0-07-139597-0 (paperback)

This book was set in Bembo
Printed and bound by Lake Book Manufacturing

Cover design by Nick Panos
Cover photograph copyright © Stone/Robert Daly
Author photograph by David Carlson

McGraw-Hill books are available at special quantity discounts to use as premiums and sales
promotions, or for use in corporate training programs. For more information, please write to the
Director of Special Sales, Professional Publishing, McGraw-Hill, Two Penn Plaza, New York, NY
10121-2298. Or contact your local bookstore.

This book is printed on acid-free paper.

## Advance Praise for *Mind Gym*

*"For the past eight years Gary "Bat" Mack has been a great help to me and my teams.* Mind Gym *can help you whether you're a player, coach, or manager."*
>—LOU PINIELLA, MANAGER, SEATTLE MARINERS

*"Gary Mack draws from decades of expertise and research to provide the most precious gems of performance wisdom. This book will help you perform optimally under pressure and overcome adversities along the way."*
>—PAUL G. STOLTZ, PH.D., AUTHOR OF NATIONAL
>BESTSELLER *ADVERSITY QUOTIENT*

*"I believe building mental muscle is just as important as physical muscle to be a champion. This book belongs in every gym bag."*
>—BILL PEARL, MR. UNIVERSE AND
>WBBA HALL OF FAME

*"Once I started reading* Mind Gym *I couldn't put it down. It's what we're all about at the Grand Canyon State Games, which is competition for everyone regardless of age or ability. Anyone who competes will receive something positive from this book."*
>—ERIK WIDMARK, CEO, GRAND CANYON STATE GAMES

*"As the father of an MVP, I recommend this book to all parents interested in helping their children reach their full potential on and off the field."*
>—KEN GRIFFEY SR., ALL-STAR AND CEO OF
>GRIFFEY INTERNATIONAL

*"A home run, touchdown, and slam-dunk all in one."*
>—BOB KRIEGEL, BESTSELLING AUTHOR AND CO-AUTHOR
>OF *INNER SKIING* WITH TIM GALLWEY

"*Everyone receives a certain amount of God-given ability. Our job, as athletes, is to get the most out of that talent. This book provides excellent teachings in training one's mind to reach and maintain peak performance.*"
—MIKE NEIL, GOLD MEDAL WINNER, SYDNEY OLYMPIC GAMES, SUMMER 2000

"*Who would think mental aspects could be so much fun? This is the simplest, most accurate and entertaining mental coaching book available. It's fun to read and easy to understand.*"
—JIM COLBORN, MAJOR LEAGUE ALL-STAR AND PITCHING COACH

"*As an avid golfer, I recommend this book to anyone desiring to raise their productivity or to lower their handicap.*"
—DAN QUAYLE, 4-HANDICAPPER AND FORMER VICE PRESIDENT OF THE UNITED STATES

"Mind Gym *is another example of Gary's ability to use stories to coach us through the challenges that life sends our way. It is filled with suggestions that will make athletes, firefighters, teachers, artists, and everyone more positive, productive, and healthy in their personal and work lives. This book will make you a better performer in the "game of life."*"
—DENNIS COMPTON, FIRE CHIEF AND AUTHOR OF THE WHEN IN DOUBT, LEAD BOOK SERIES

"*Whether it's board room or locker room, the formula for success is the same.* Mind Gym *not only should be required reading for every aspiring athlete, but everyone who wishes to excel in their chosen field. I have successfully applied many of the concepts discussed in the book to the operation of our own financial institution.*"
—DAVID HIGHMARK, CHAIRMAN AND CEO, NORTHERN TRUST BANK OF ARIZONA

# CONTENTS

Foreword  ix

PART I  WELCOME TO THE INNER GAME
Yogi Was Right  3
Mind Games  8
The Head Edge  13
The Pressure Principle  18
Mental Toughness  24
Know Your Numbers  29
Responsibility Psychology  35
Getting Over Yourself  40
The Next Level  47

PART II  LIVING THE DREAM
Good Enough to Dream  55
Progress Not Perfection  60
Don't Shirk the Work  65
Fatal Distractions  70
Fate Loves the Fearless  76
Permission to Win  81

The Fire Inside  87

The Four D's  92

PART III  MIND-SET FOR SUCCESS

Attitude Is Everything  99

Riding the Pines  104

You Gotta Believe  108

Between the Ears  114

Servant or Master  119

Fear Lives in the Future  125

Breathe and Focus  130

Be Here, Now  135

Hurry, Slowly  140

Try Easier  145

Simply Observe  150

The Bottom Line  155

PART IV  IN THE ZONE

Trust Your Stuff  163

White Moments  168

Paralysis by Analysis  174

Paradoxes of Performances  180

Choice Not Chance  186

Inner Excellence 191

The Hero Within 197

The Well-Played Game 202

Game Day 207

The Mirror Test 212

The Big Win 220

# FOREWORD

When I was nine years old growing up in Miami, I dreamed of being a major league baseball player someday. The dream was a little blurry back then, and it disappeared when I quit baseball and took up basketball. I wanted to become the next Magic Johnson or the next Larry Bird. Then one day I was talking with my mother and my older brother, and I realized that there aren't too many Dominicans playing in the NBA. So after a two-year layoff, I started playing baseball again, and that picture in my head, that dream, came back to me. That blurry image started taking focus.

I can tell you I wouldn't be where I am now if I hadn't seen myself wearing a big-league uniform long before it happened. I believe in the power of dreams.

I also believe mental preparation goes hand-in-hand with setting goals and hard work. The way I use my mind is the biggest reason I've been able to enjoy success and play at a high level in a game where you have to prove yourself every day. In sports, as in life, talent will take you just so far. I try to attain goals *mentally* first. Let me give you an example. I don't want to sound cocky, but early in the 1996 season, I visualized winning the American League Most Valuable Player award and holding it above my head. I visioned winning the batting title and holding up that trophy, too. I visioned a .380 batting average. In my mind I could see the number, flashing and blinking on exit signs . . . .380 . . . .380 . . . .380.

That year I missed winning the MVP by three votes and won the batting title. Playing the game was the easy part. The real work was in the preparation. What I did in May paid off with rewards in November.

Just as I believe in dreams, I believe in the power of positive reinforcement and visualization. Some nights when I go to bed I will tell myself, maybe 150 times, "I hit the ball solid. I hit the ball solid. What do I do for a living? I hit the ball solid." I see the results from my mind's eye out. I see myself from the fans' perspective. From the manager's view in the dugout. I picture myself on the field from different angles. I believe a champion wins in his mind first, then he plays the game, not the other way around. It's powerful stuff.

My season is long, extending from spring training through 162 games and the playoffs. Every athlete in every sport experiences peaks and valleys. During tough times I don't worry. I don't judge my performance by results. Most important is my physical and mental preparation. The question I ask when I look in the mirror is "Am I ready to play?" If the answer is yes, I feel confident. Once the ball is thrown, or it's hit, the outcome is out of your control.

I have known Gary Mack as a team counselor and as a friend since 1993 when I became a professional baseball player. *Mind Gym* takes you into the hearts and minds of many of the world's greatest athletes and coaches and illustrates the importance of the inner game. The lessons and mental skills you will learn by reading these pages are the same ones I use on a daily basis. Whether you're a big leaguer, or a Little Leaguer, or in whatever game you play, Gary and this book can help take your game to the next level.

ALEX RODRIGUEZ

# PART I

# WELCOME TO THE INNER GAME

# YOGI WAS RIGHT

*Ninety percent of the game is half mental.*

—YOGI BERRA

*You have to train your mind like you train your body.*

—BRUCE JENNER

When Yogi Berra became manager of the Yankees, a reporter asked if he had enough experience to handle the job. "Sure," Berra said. "I've been playing eighteen years, and you can observe a lot just by watching." Closing his notebook, the writer walked away wearing the same look of faint bewilderment that the waitress had after she asked Yogi if he wanted his pizza cut into four slices or eight.

"Better make it four," Yogi decided. "I dunno if I can eat eight."

In working with elite athletes and professional sports teams, I often begin my counseling sessions and presentations by quoting Yogi's wit and wisdom. A favorite line, one certain to get a laugh, is Yogi's mathematical observation that 90 percent of the game is half mental.

But let me ask a question. Have you ever thought seriously about that famous Yogi-ism? How much of the game—*your* game—is mental?

Maybe I can lead you to an answer. Let's begin with an exercise I introduced to an international group of sports psychologists, Olympic and professional athletes, coaches, musicians, dancers, astronauts, doctors, lawyers, and fire chiefs in Ottawa, Canada. After completing this exercise and answering the questions, I think you will discover what the world's greatest athletes and the most successful people in other walks of life know to be true—that once you reach a certain level of competency, the mental skills become as important to performance as the physical skills, if not more so.

Now, sit back. Relax. Begin to recall the sights and sounds and feelings of you performing at your very best. In your mind's eye, imagine your best day ever. Picture that time when you were at the top of your game, when every move and decision you made was the right one, when it seemed like every break went your way. Some athletes and performers describe their best-day experience as "playing in the zone." I call those sweet spots in time "white moments," which we will explore later.

Imagine you are watching your own highlights film. You feel no fear, no anxieties, and no self-doubts. Everything is flowing and going your way. Look around. Where are you? What time of day is it? What time of year? What are you wearing? Who is with you? Who is watching? What do you hear? Breathe in the air. If you are on a playing field, or a golf course, can you smell the grass? Visualize that pleasurable experience.

Now, let that image slowly fade, and in its place recall your worst performance. Think of the game, event, or experience when you felt weak and ineffective, when nothing went your way no matter how hard you tried. Now leave that memory behind. Fast-forward to the present.

With Yogi's quote in mind, compare yourself competing at your best and at your worst. Then honestly answer these questions: What percentage of the difference in those performances had to do with your physical skills? What percentage was *mental*?

When working with a team of professional athletes, I have everyone in the clubhouse stand. I ask if the mental part of their performance was less than 10 percent. If so, I tell them to sit down. Those who think it was less than 20 percent are asked to take a seat. "How about those of you," I ask, "who think the mental game was less than 30 percent? Sit down. How about less than 40 percent?"

At 50 percent, at least half the room is still standing. Would you be standing, too?

If the answer is yes, this is my next question: If you believe the difference between your best and worst performance was, as Yogi said, at least 50 percent mental, then how much time do you spend on the mental game? How many books about sports psychology have you read? How many lessons have you taken from a "head" coach?

As you demonstrated in the exercise, the mind is like a VCR. It records sights and sounds, and the tape plays continuously. The human body treats every vivid thought and image as if it is real and happening now. Everyone who has awakened from a nightmare knows this to be true.

Studies have proven that mental training will not only enhance performance and improve productivity but also add to your enjoyment. Whatever your age, whatever your game, you can learn how to use your mind more constructively. You can learn how to stay focused. You can learn to deal with adversity. Stay motivated during difficult times. Avoid fatal distractions. You can learn how to follow your dreams and live your life on purpose.

Achieving inner excellence is a process. Building mental muscle, like building physical muscle, requires time and effort. The more you work on the inside, the more it will show on the outside. First you must make a commitment. As Yogi supposedly said, when you come to the fork in the road, take it. By reading the first section, you are taking your first step.

Think of the book in your hands as your mind gym. Read the lessons, do the exercises, and answer the questions. If you do, you will acquire the skills needed to create the ideal mental state that will allow you to rise to the next level and perform at your best by choice rather than chance.

*What you think affects how you feel and perform. Training your brain is as important as training your body.*

# MIND GAMES

*The mind messes up more shots than the body.*

—Tommy Bolt

*The mind is a powerful thing and most people don't use it properly.*

—Mark McGwire

Gene Stallings stood on the practice field, arms folded across his chest. The Arizona Cardinals were at summer training camp in Flagstaff, and every player could feel the stoic presence of the team's tall, tough-minded head coach.

Stallings is a protégé of the late Paul "Bear" Bryant. He played for Bryant at Texas A&M and served seven seasons as an assistant to the coaching legend at Alabama. Like Bryant, Stallings valued practice time. He placed a premium on mental toughness and the work habits of his players. Now here he stood, casting a long shadow, his steely gaze fixed on a placekicker as he swung his right foot, soccer-style, into and through the ball. When the field-goal attempt sailed wildly wide of the mark—the kicker shanked the ball—Stallings's face hardened like ready-mix cement. In disgust, he turned his back and walked away, muttering under his breath.

Once Gene was out of earshot, I drew the kicker aside. "What happened?" I asked. This was my first season as team counselor for the NFL club.

"Mack, I'm a *great* field goal kicker," the player said with conviction. Then he thought of his coach and his glacial stare. He shook his head. "But I just can't kick when Gene's watching me."

"Well, you know," I said, gently, unable to suppress a smile, "I think he's going to be at all the games."

The kicker had plenty of leg, and distance was no problem. But he had allowed himself to become self-conscious and coach-conscious rather than task-conscious. His mind was on his boss. If the player expected better results, he had to change his thought patterns. He needed to work on the mental part of his game.

One key to achieving success in sports is learning how to focus on the task and not let negative thoughts intrude. The mind can concentrate on only one thing at a time. So, rather than suppress what you don't want to happen, you must focus on what you *do* want to happen or on some neutral thought. In working with placekickers, I use a distraction technique. I ask them to create a word that, when said to themselves, will block out all negative thought and help relieve tension. Al Del Greco, a veteran kicker for the Tennessee Titans who played in Super Bowl

XXXIV, has his own word: "birdie." Al is a scratch golfer, perhaps the best golfer in the National Football League. For him "birdie" creates the feeling of success and reminds him of the fun he has on the golf course.

The brain is like a megacomputer that controls the body. Herbert Benson, a Harvard cardiologist, found that having patients focus on their breathing and repeating the word "one" lowered their blood pressure and heart rate. Try it yourself.

The brain can do remarkable things but, unlike a computer, it doesn't come with an instruction manual. Unfortunately, too often we pull up the wrong "programs" at the wrong times.

This section begins with a profound quote from Tommy Bolt, the former professional golfer. Terrible Tommy, he was called. Thunder Bolt. The joke was that Bolt was bilingual—fluent in English and profanity. His temper and club-throwing tantrums are part of golf's rich lore. According to legend, after lipping out six putts in a row during one tournament round, Bolt shook his fist at the heavens and shouted, "Why don't You come down and fight like a man?!"

But Bolt understood the power of the mind and how the brain can sabotage performance. When a weekend golfer arrives at a water hole what is the second thing he does after fishing an old ball—a water ball—out of his bag? Stepping to the tee he tells himself, "*Don't* hit it in the water." What we've learned in psychology is that actions follow our thoughts and images. If you say, "Don't hit it in the water" and you're looking at the water, you have just programmed your mind to send the ball to a watery grave. The law of dominant thought says your mind is going to remember the most dominant thought. Think water, remember water, and water likely is what you will get.

Rather than say "Don't hit it in the water," try another instruction, like "Land the ball ten yards to the right of the pin." You get what your mind sets. The mind works most effectively when you're telling it what to do rather than what not to do.

When I was with the Chicago Cubs, a starting pitcher telephoned me from Montreal. He had been rocked in his last outing. In an almost pleading voice, he said he needed help. When I asked him to relate the conversation he had with himself when he was alone on the mound, struggling to find the plate, he ticked off a laundry list of negative thoughts: "Don't hang your curve. Don't walk this guy. The ump won't give me a call. If I don't get through the fifth inning I'm going to lose my spot in the rotation."

I give athletes I work with a three-by-five card. On one side I have them list their personal keys to success; on the other, their performance keys to success. I asked the Cubs pitcher to tell me his performance keys to success. "What are you doing when you're really on your game?"

"I'm locating my fastball," he replied. "I'm throwing first-pitch strikes. I'm changing speed."

"So how do you do those things?" I asked.

"Good balance," he said. "Shoulder back. Drive through."

"Good," I told him. "In five days you start against the Mets in New York. All I want you to do before the game is to focus on those three things."

In his next appearance, the pitcher threw a complete-game shutout. In less than a week he couldn't have changed that much physically. His turnaround is proof that by changing your thinking—and you *can* choose how you think—you can change your performance. Put another way, if you don't like the program you are watching, switch the channel.

*Learn to use your mind or your mind will use you. Actions follow our thoughts and images. Don't look where you don't want to go.*

# THE HEAD EDGE

*The whole idea is to get an edge. Sometimes it takes just a little extra something to get that edge, but you have to have it.*
—DON SHULA

*The most important part of a player's body is above his shoulders.*
—TY COBB

Moments before his last at-bat of the 1998 season, baseball's new Man of Steel sat in the shadows of the St. Louis dugout with his eyes closed. Mark McGwire wasn't napping. The man with the broad shoulders and Popeye forearms, who had already hit one home run that late September afternoon, was deep in thought—mentally rehearsing.

"It's hard work, mentally and physically," the Cardinals slugger once said of the art of hitting. "Everybody looks at my body, but I use my mind more than my arms."

By the time McGwire stepped into the batter's box he was focused, relaxed, and ready. When Montreal relief pitcher Carl Pavano turned loose a 95-mph fastball, Big Mac's mind and body worked as one. A ripping swing. A cork-popping sound. Away it went, a streaking line drive. The ball landed in the left-field stands for home run number seventy—proving to the last skeptic that Big Mac's sixty-nine others that season weren't flukes.

McGwire hit five home runs in the last forty-four hours of the season and waved good-bye to Sammy Sosa, with whom he had formed a mutual admiration club and competed in a dinger derby unlike anything baseball had ever seen.

Sports psychology has been called the science of success because it studies what successful people do. What we have found—and what McGwire and other great athletes validate—is the value of mental rehearsal and imagery.

Here is how Carl Yastrzemski described his use of imagery: "The night before a game, I visualize the pitcher and the pitches I'm going to see the next day. I hit the ball right on the button. I know what it's going to feel like. I hit the pitches where I want to."

The power of visualization and mental rehearsal has been demonstrated in dozens of research studies. If you take twenty athletes of equal ability and give ten mental training they will outperform the ten who received no mental training every time. This is what we call the head edge.

One interesting study involved college basketball players. For three months, one group shot free throws for one hour each day. Another group spent an hour each day thinking about shooting free throws. The third group shot baskets thirty minutes a day and spent thirty minutes visualizing the ball going through the hoop from the foul line. Which group, at the end of the study, do you think improved its free-throw shooting the most? The third group did. The imagery had as much impact on accuracy as shooting baskets.

In another case study, cited in *Foundations of Sport and Exercise Psychology*, a sports psychologist worked with the United States Olympic ski team. He divided the team into two groups equally matched for ski-racing ability. One group received imagery training; the other served as a control group. The coach quickly realized that the skiers practicing imagery were improving more rapidly than those in the control group. He called off the experiment and insisted that all his skiers be given the opportunity to train using imagery.

As a kid growing up in an immigrant neighborhood in Queens, New York, I played on a soccer team in the Polish American Youth League. One Saturday we went to Randalls Island for a clinic. I sat in wonder in the presence of Pelé, the greatest soccer player in the world.

I still remember what he said: enthusiasm and the mental edge are the keys to winning. Pelé described his routine, which was the same for every game he played. An hour before he stepped onto the field, Pelé went into the locker room, picked up two towels, and retreated to a private corner. Stretching out, he placed one towel under the back of his head, like a pillow. He covered his eyes with the other. Then he began to roll his mental camera. In his mind's eye he saw himself as a youngster playing soccer on the beaches of Brazil. He could feel the gentle breeze. He could smell the salt air. He remembered how much fun he had and how much he loved the game.

Pele then hit the fast-forward button of his mental video. He began recalling his greatest moments in the World Cup and reliving that winning feeling. Then he let those images fade and began rehearsing for the upcoming game. He pictured his opponents. He saw himself dribbling through defenders, heading shots, and scoring goals. After a half-hour in solitude, alone with his thoughts and the slide show of positive images, Pele did his stretching exercises. When he trotted into the stadium, washed in cheers, he knew he was physically and mentally prepared.

An exercise for this section is called the mind gym. When I was with the Cubs, the team acquired Bob Tewksbury from the Yankees. At the time Bob wasn't a dominating big-league pitcher. He didn't have a great fastball, relying instead on location and changes in speed. In working together, I asked Bob to create his own mind gym, an imaginary retreat where he could go before games to reflect and mentally prepare. His vivid imagination created an elaborate studio. Bob's mind gym featured a bubble-like structure—an energy machine with a ticker tape that flashed positive affirmations, and a state-of-the-art sound system. From his mind-gym bed Bob could stretch out and watch a highlights tape of himself on a big-screen TV mounted overhead. Tewskbury later bloomed into an All-Star with the Cardinals.

To get the head edge, try creating your own mind gym. You always can do mental practice, even when you are physically tired or injured. Make your images as vivid and as clear as you can. See yourself overcoming mistakes, and imagine yourself doing things well. Remember, confidence comes from knowing you are mentally and physically prepared.

*Sports psychology is the science of success. Studies show that within a group of athletes of equal ability, those who receive mental training outperform those who don't almost every time. Mental skills, like physical skills, need constant practice.*

# THE PRESSURE PRINCIPLE

*Under pressure you can perform fifteen percent better or worse.*
—SCOTT HAMILTON

*When you have fun, it changes all the pressure into pleasure.*
—KEN GRIFFEY SR. *and* KEN GRIFFEY JR.

He was a sickly child, his growth stunted by a rare digestive disease. Kids at school called him "Peanut" and other hurtful names. A figure-skating judge said he was too small to succeed in international competition. But now here he was, on center stage, at five-foot-three, 115 pounds, the biggest attraction of the Winter Olympics. Figure skating is the main event of the Winter Games. It is rich theater, made-for-TV drama. The anticipation is delicious. For the performers the pressure is palpable. One tiny mistake—one fraction of a point deducted by unforgiving judges—can mean the difference between triumph and tears.

Scott Hamilton stood alone in the spotlight. In 1980 the American skater had finished fifth at the Games in

Lake Placid. Now, after four years of working on eliminating his weaknesses in training, after four years of waiting and dreaming, this was his chance, perhaps his last chance, to win an Olympic gold medal. Hamilton took a deep breath and launched body and soul into his routine. He glided, jumped, and spun. Arms outstretched, he became one with the music, his flashing skate blades cutting stencils in the ice.

Four minutes later it was over. Bravos filled the arena, and bouquets tossed from the stands littered the ice. The applause sounded like hard rain.

Hamilton reminded us that winners come in all sizes. Wearing a shiny gold medal that hung almost to his waist, the American Olympic champion lived his dream. That night in Sarajevo he credited his success to his mental preparedness. "Under pressure," Hamilton said, "people can perform fifteen percent better or fifteen percent worse."

I was among the millions of TV viewers who witnessed Hamilton's performance that night. The skater's comment intrigued me. All of us are performers in the game of life. We face pressure and competition every day—at work, in the boardroom, in the classroom, on the golf course, on the tennis court, the basketball court, and at play.

With Hamilton's quote in mind, I began a new career studying the psychology of stress and the psychology of success. My mission was to learn all I could about playing under pressure. I wanted to find out why, under pressure, some athletes break through, as Hamilton did, while others break down. In what ways, and to what extent, does the mind influence how we perform?

What is pressure? Golfer Lee Trevino said, "Pressure is when you've got thirty-five bucks riding on a four-foot putt and you've only got five dollars in your pocket." Former Pittsburgh Steelers coach Chuck Noll defined pressure as "something you feel only when you don't know what you're doing."

During the late stages of a pennant race, former Montreal pitcher Bill Lee was asked how much pressure he was feeling. Never one to duck a question, baseball's space cadet thought a moment, then announced, "Thirty-two pounds per square inch, at sea level." Charles Barkley, the former NBA star, glibly dismisses the subject, saying "Pressure is what you put in tires." But pressure is real. Pressure exists. Every athlete, whether he or she admits it, feels pressure in competition.

So where does pressure come from? Former Denver Broncos quarterback John Elway, a future NFL Hall of Famer, said he always felt the pressure to win, but most of that pressure came from within. Hockey great Mark Messier agrees: "The only pressure I'm under is the pressure I've put on myself."

The human body reacts to pressure and stress. The heart beats faster, and breathing quickens. No one is immune. Jack Nicklaus, who has won more major championships than any golfer in history, says, "Pressure creates tension, and when you're tense, you want to get your task over and done with as fast as possible. The more you hurry in golf the worse you probably will play, which leads to even heavier pressure and greater tension." Listen to tennis star Arthur Ashe: "We have a natural tendency to invest more energy when we are under pressure. But when tension rises, two things happen: the feet can't move and the diaphragm collapses. It's automatic. It's in the genetic code."

Pressure gets a bad name, but it can bring out the best in you. In fact, if you don't feel any pressure you're probably not going to do your best. Former big-league pitcher Goose Gossage thrived on pressure. "I'm not at my best," Gossage once said, "until the situation is at its worst."

I got to know Gossage when I worked with the Cubs and later the Seattle Mariners. Goose was a master at keeping his job in perspective. I remember asking him how he handled the pressure of being a closer. Gossage said, "Every time I come into a game I think of my home in the Rockies, and that relaxes me. And I tell myself the worst thing that could happen is that I'd be home fishing there tomorrow."

Hamilton dealt with pressure in another way. Sixteen years after watching him win the gold medal, I spoke with Scott when he was in Phoenix with the Stars on Ice tour. When I told him that his "fifteen percent" quote about pressure became my inspiration for writing this book the skater smiled. Hamilton said he approached his gold-medal performance in Sarajevo with "refined indifference." He had trained for years to prepare for that moment. When the spotlight came on and the music began, he let fate carry him through. The hard work was over. Now, he told himself, go out and enjoy.

Sarah Hughes chose the same approach at the 2002 Winter Games in Salt Lake City. In fourth place after the short program and feeling she had nothing to lose, the 16-year-old took a leap of faith and skated with abandon. *Sports Illustrated* described her performance as "uninhibited joy." While older, more experienced Olympians faltered under pressure, Sarah made history by landing two triple-triple combinations and won the gold. "I didn't hold back," Hughes said, beaming. "It was my greatest skate ever."

Pressure can be a positive force or a negative one. A close friend, Ken Ravizza, is one of the first sports psychologists to publish a study on the experiences of athletes during their "greatest moment" in sports. He found that more than 80 percent of the athletes said they felt no fear of failure. They weren't thinking about their performance. They were immersed in the activity. They were in "the zone." The probability of achieving the outcome you want increases when you let go of the need to have it.

Go into your mental studio, which we discussed in the last section. Recall a time when you broke through, when the pressure worked *for* you. Notice what you were doing, feeling, and saying to yourself. Were you relaxed or tense? Excited or anxious? Did you fear failure or feel a desire to win? Were you focused on the outcome or absorbed in the process?

*Everything gets interpreted. Pressure is in the brain of the beholder. Learn to view pressure as a challenge to meet rather than a threat of defeat.*

# MENTAL TOUGHNESS

*The most important attribute a player must have is mental toughness.*

—MIA HAMM

*Competitive toughness is an acquired skill and not an inherited gift.*

—CHRIS EVERT

When Joe Bugel coached the Arizona Cardinals, the highest praise he could bestow upon a player was to call him an "LTG," short for Legitimate Tough Guy. An LTG is a fierce competitor, a battler, an athlete who looks at pressure as a challenge, who refuses to lose, and never, ever quits. An example of an LTG in another sport is the soccer player who once had the ball stolen during a scrimmage. As the defender turned upfield, the player who lost the ball began yanking on the thief's jersey and didn't let go until he fell to the ground, his shirt half off. He lay there, grinning in disbelief and admiration at the girl who had fouled him and then walked away without a glance back.

Her name is Mariel Margaret Hamm. The highest-scoring woman in the history of international soccer is the definition of mental toughness. Shy by nature and labeled a reluctant star, Mia told her teammates, "Nothing stands between us and success but our will to win." It was Mia who said, "Our warrior mentality means that once we step on the field, we are coming after you with a 'take no prisoners' attitude."

The U.S. women's soccer team was the sports story of the year in 1999. The Americans won the World Cup, outlasting China in a final game that featured two exhausting overtimes and a dramatic shootout. If Mia Hamm wasn't the heart of her team, then she was the left ventricle.

In this section we will define the seven characteristics of mental toughness. They are a set of behaviors and beliefs about yourself, your work, your sport, and how you interact. A person who is mentally tough looks at competition as a challenge to rise up to rather than a threat to back down from. Like physical skills, mental toughness can be learned through quality instruction and practice.

**Competitive.** Professional golfer Nancy Lopez clearly defines a competitor. "A competitor will find a way to win," she said. "Competitors take bad breaks and use them to drive themselves just that much harder. Quitters take bad breaks and use them as reasons to give up." Michael Jordan's flirtation with a major-league baseball career is testimony to his competitive fire. Why would the greatest basketball player in history attempt to play another sport? Because he couldn't accept not trying. Late in life, Joe DiMaggio said he would give away all his trophies and records to be twenty-five years old and able to compete again. "The one thing I both loved and now miss the most," DiMaggio said, "was the competition."

**Confident.** Tiger Woods said, "Every time I play, in my own mind I'm the favorite." Confident athletes have a can-do attitude, a belief they can handle whatever comes their way. They almost never fall victim to self-defeating thoughts. Jordan said he went into every game believing he was the best player on the court until someone proved otherwise. Very few did.

**Control.** Successful athletes are able to control their emotions and behavior. They focus on what they can control and don't allow things that are out of their control to affect them. The hallmark of mentally tough athletes is the ability to maintain poise, concentration, and emotional control under the greatest pressure and the most challenging situations.

**Committed.** Mentally tough athletes focus their time and energy on their goals and dreams. They are self-directed and highly motivated. Listen to John McEnroe: "There are scores of players who can hit every shot in the book who never make it into a Grand Slam event. Those who make it are there because they are mentally tougher. They *wanted* it more." After his free fall from the top of the tennis rankings, Andre Agassi rededicated himself to the game. He worked hard to get back into shape. The results speak for themselves.

**Composure.** Mentally tough athletes know how to stay focused and deal with adversity. In working with hockey teams, I'll sometimes approach a player in the locker room and give him a shove when he isn't looking. I want to see his reaction. Oftentimes the player will instinctively make a fist and draw back his arm, ready to throw a punch. In hockey and basketball the athlete who retaliates is usually the one who gets penalized. I tell tennis players they can expect two or three bad calls in every match, sometimes more. How they manage their emotions can determine whether they win or lose. A mentally tough player will say to himself, "OK, if I've got to beat the other guy *and* the referee, then fine—I'll do that." The motto I give to firefighters in the Phoenix Fire Department also applies to you: keep your cool when the heat is on.

**Courage.** A mentally tough athlete must be willing to take a risk. That's what peak performers do. In the book *Adversity Quotient* author Paul Stoltz compares success with a mountain. Only climbers get to the top. The campers, those who get part of the way up and decide to stay where they are, will never feel as alive or as proud as the climbers. As the philosopher said, it takes courage to grow up and to achieve your full potential.

**Consistency.** Mentally tough athletes possess an inner strength. They often play their best when they're feeling their worst. They don't make excuses.

*Competition is won or lost on the six-inch playing field between the ears. Practice the seven C's of mental toughness. Learn to love the competition.*

# KNOW YOUR NUMBERS

*In a close game I check my pulse. I know if it gets over one hundred it's going to affect my thinking.*
—PHIL JACKSON

*Mentally I try to stay at a medium level, not too high or too low.*
—TODD ZEILE

In graduate school the most important psychological concept I learned is something called the performance curve. Draw an upside down "U." To the left draw a vertical line, and connect it to a horizontal line drawn beneath the inverted "U." Number both lines incrementally from zero to ten. The horizontal line represents stress and arousal; the vertical line represents performance and productivity.

As athletes become stimulated their numbers on both lines increase. When they achieve peak efficiency—when they are performing at their best, physically and mentally—they are at the top of the human function curve, at the apex of the inverted "U."

Everyone has an optimal number that corresponds with peak performance. I tell all athletes I work with that they need to "know their numbers." They also need to recognize their early warning signs. Imagine you are a car. How many rpms should you be producing so your motor is running smoothly and efficiently, not chugging along too slowly but also not going over the red line?

An athlete's ideal numbers—the optimal level of performance—depend upon (1) his or her temperament; (2) the time or length of the event; and (3) the nature of the task. A sprinter wouldn't have the same number as a marathon runner because the time of the event is different. A basketball center whose job is muscling opponents under the basket would have a different number than, say, a three-point shooter. This also is true of starting pitchers and relievers. The nature of their task is different.

Athletes have different emotional makeups. Some are more high-strung than others. To use the car analogy, one athlete might be a Porsche, another a pickup truck. Just as it's important to know what to do when your vehicle's oil or brake light comes on, it's important to recognize your own early warning signals.

When I was with the Cubs, I taught a class on the mental aspects of performing along with former major league pitcher Jim Colborn. To illustrate what I meant by early warning signs, I would look around the room in the church basement where we met and select one of the pitchers to come to the front of the class and read a chapter of the manual aloud. With some, all you had to do was *look* at them. Hoping they wouldn't be summoned, they shrank before my eyes. One of the greatest fears many people have is the fear of public speaking.

Under stress, some people are cardiac responders—their heart rate goes up. Some are skin responders—they begin to perspire. Others begin to breathe rapidly, feel their stomachs churn, or feel their neck and back muscles tensing. These are all physical early warning signs. Mentally our minds start racing. A little voice begins whispering negative thoughts.

Not long ago I received a phone call from an executive of a National Hockey League team. He told me about one of the club's top prospects, a promising high-round draft choice who had struggled during his rookie year.

"This guy should be making millions," the executive said. "And he's only making thousands." By that, he meant the player, for whatever reason, was under-performing. He had not begun to tap his potential. I agreed to meet with the rookie before the club sent him down to the minor leagues.

In our first session, the player confessed he felt a lot of pressure being a high-round draft pick. Whenever the game started he became overly excited. During his first shift on the ice he over-skated the puck. His passes were too long. He lost his composure around the net. After we talked about the performance curve I asked him, "What number are you?"

"I'm a nine, or a ten," he said. "Sometimes I feel like I'm an eleven."

"What's your number when you're playing at your best?" I asked.

"I'm a six, or a seven."

When the puck dropped, the young player's tachometer was already hitting the red line. Unhappy with the rookie's performance, the coach benched him. Later, when the rookie returned to the game after sitting out several shifts, he said he felt a half-step slow. His legs were heavy. He missed passes. It was as if he couldn't get up to speed.

"What's your number then?" I asked.

"Three or four," he replied. "Maybe five."

To help him calm down before games, we changed his routine. In the locker room the young player began listening to slower music. During games, I instructed him to pretend he was going in with each shift change. By mentally skating every shift, he was better able to focus on the action and the opponent. Once he returned to the ice he performed at six or seven—his peak performance number.

I told him that performance is like the guitar he plays for relaxation. If the strings are too loose the music is flat. If they're too tight, they could snap. Just as the instrument's strings need to be at the right tension, an athlete must have his body tuned for the right performance.

Whenever I think of over-revving, I am reminded of Dexter Manley. In 1991 after his drug suspension, the former All Pro with the Washington Redskins joined the Arizona Cardinals. On the day of the Cowboys game in Irving, Texas, a team doctor came to me.

"Mack, you've got to go in there." I could hear the concern in his voice. He motioned anxiously toward the training room. "It's Dexter."

Although we had known each other only a few weeks, Dexter and I enjoyed a good relationship. I liked him and believed he trusted me. When I entered the inner sanctum of the training room, Manley was the picture of pent-up emotion, as high-strung as a thoroughbred lathering in the paddock before the start of a race. His vacant eyes said he wasn't at home. Dexter was in another world.

"Dexter. Dexter!" Slowly, I got his attention. As Manley began to settle down, I looked him in the eye and asked what was going on. What was he thinking about?

As kickoff neared, Manley said he pictured himself back in the Third Ward in Houston, the poor neighborhood where he grew up. "Mack, I don't *ever* want to be there again." In an attempt to "psyche" himself up for the game, Manley had become over-aroused, which can be counterproductive in an athlete. Even though Dexter was a great pass rusher, the Cardinals didn't want to put him into the game on third down in short-yardage situations for fear he would jump offside and give the other team a free first down.

The two cases illustrate the importance of the performance curve and knowing your numbers. A quote to remember came from former big-league pitcher Carl Hubbell, who invented the screwball. Hubbell said, "I had no chance of controlling a ball game until I first controlled myself."

*You can't control your performance until you are in control of yourself. What you're thinking. How you're feeling. Most importantly, your physiology. Know your numbers and your early warning signs.*

# RESPONSIBILITY
# PSYCHOLOGY

*What has benefited me the most is learning I can't control what happens outside of my pitching.*
—GREG MADDUX

*My message is simple: take control of your life.*
—CHARLES BARKLEY

In 1989 Greg Maddux was struggling. The young Cubs pitcher who had attended some of my classes during the fall instructional league lost five of six decisions. His earned run average soared. After watching Maddux get roughed up, I made a promise to myself. If Greg didn't show improvement in his first outing after the All-Star break I was going to call him, which I did.

The transformation that followed the break was astounding. Beginning on July 23, Maddux won five in a row. On August 7 his complete-game victory over Montreal lifted the Cubs into first place in the division—where they stayed the remainder of the regular season.

A lot of people asked me, "What did you tell him?"

Nothing.

When I called, Greg wasn't home.

Sports psychology doesn't create talent. It only can help release it. Sharing the story is my way of being responsible, our topic in this section. In sports, as in life, your future and success depend upon many things, but mostly they depend upon you. You have the responsibility to shape your life. You are the person who pushes yourself forward or holds yourself back. The power to succeed or fail is yours alone.

I like what Don Sutton, the Hall of Fame pitcher, said: "I think the reason for my success is that I was raised as a member of a sharecropping family in the South, and I had to take responsibility early in life."

One of the great powers we have is the power to choose. How you choose to look at an event is going to affect how you feel and how you perform. I see a tendency in young pitchers to get upset with umpires or teammates who make infield mistakes. Too often, people play the blame game. Successful people take responsibility for themselves and their game. They understand that it's not the event but how they respond to it that's most important.

You have the choice how you will respond to any situation. People with inner excellence, like Greg Maddux, focus on what they can control. Maddux doesn't have a Hall of Fame build. "I don't look like a baseball player. I mean, look at me," the bespectacled Atlanta right-hander says. But Maddux, the most dominant pitcher of his generation, has a Hall of Fame brain.

Maddux knows the only things he can control during a game are himself and his pitches. Tim Salmon, a former American League rookie of the year, said, "I can't control the pitcher, the ball, the fielders, or the crowd, so I must be in control of myself."

The great Stan Musial said, "When a pitcher's throwing a spitball, don't worry. Don't complain. Just hit the dry side, like I do."

During spring training in 1994, I gave a talk to the Seattle Mariners' pitching staff. The lesson that day was about responsibility psychology. Gathered on the bright-green grass field at the club's new complex in Peoria, Arizona, I shared Maddux's quote. I reminded the players that while they can't always control what happens, they can always control how they respond to it.

After the speech, my cell phone rang.

I recognized the Oklahoma accent immediately. It was Buddy Ryan, the new head coach of the NFL Cardinals. As the Cardinals' team counselor for six years, I had met Buddy a few weeks earlier at the NFL scouting combine in Indianapolis. In hopes of making a good impression, I conducted a series of video interviews with prospective draft choices at the combine.

"Gary, can you stop by today?"

"Sure, Buddy," I said. "Be there in an hour."

Leaving Peoria, I turned my car south toward the Cardinals complex in Tempe. Buddy's call had left me in good spirits. I was proud of the video interviews and felt they would be a useful player-evaluation tool for the new coach who had come to the Cardinals from the Houston Oilers. In Houston, Buddy had made national headlines after he threw a punch at fellow assistant coach Kevin Gilbride while the two were on the sideline during a game.

Buddy made big news again when he arrived in Arizona and announced, "You've got a winner in town!" I was eager to hear his plans for the upcoming season.

Ryan greeted me outside his office. It was St. Patrick's Day. He wore a green necktie, and a green carnation bloomed from his jacket lapel. Ruddy-faced, eyes twinkling, and all smiles, Buddy looked as Irish as Finian's Rainbow.

Inside his office, where I had spent many hours with his predecessor Joe Bugel, Buddy plopped down behind his giant desk. I took a seat across from him.

"Gary, I've talked to the coaches. They've got a lot of respect for you," Buddy said. I was beaming, inside and out. "The players like you. They trust you. I've heard nothing but good things. But I'm letting you go."

Boom. I felt as if I had been slapped. My heart sank. The big smile fell off my face. As I sat in stunned silence, shock and disappointment suddenly gave way to a rush of anger. *This isn't fair*, I thought. I felt my jaw tighten and my fists clench. For an instant, I pictured myself flying across the desk and delivering to my ex-boss the same kind of statement Ryan had delivered to Gilbride during a flash of anger in the heat of a big game.

Then I caught myself. An hour earlier, I had been standing in the warm sunshine in Peoria, lecturing a group of major league pitchers on being responsible. I had told them they can't always control the situation. All they can control is how they respond to it. Forcing myself, I sat back in my chair. I took a deep breath and looked Ryan in the eye.

"Buddy, I really wish you had taken the time to get to know me," I heard myself saying in a level voice. "I think I can help you and the team. But I understand. I want to wish you good luck."

We stood and shook hands.

"You still gonna be a Cardinals fan?" Ryan asked.

I told him I would. Then I left his office, consciously holding my head high. I had to walk my talk, although at that moment it wasn't easy to do.

*While you can't always control what happens, you always can control how you respond to it. It's not the situation but how you respond to it that makes the difference.*

# GETTING OVER YOURSELF

*I worked very hard. I felt I could play the game. The only thing that could stop me was myself.*
—JIM ABBOTT

*This ability to conquer oneself is no doubt the most precious of all things sports bestows on us.*
—OLGA KORBUT

Rafael Colon is my bilingual counselor for the Mariners and president of Voices Internacional. On his voice mail is this message: "To achieve anything you want in life you must first start by getting out of your own way."

Robert Kelly's *Pogo* cartoon puts it another way: "We have met the enemy and they is us."

Working in the field of sports psychology, I am fascinated by how many people defeat themselves and sabotage success. Athletes at every level often interfere with their own performance. They get in their own way with their fears, their doubts, and their self-condemning nature.

In 1994 pitcher Shawn Estes underwent surgery on his left shoulder, but his problems in the Mariners organization went beyond injuries. "When I did well, I didn't give myself enough credit," he said. "When I did badly, I beat myself up for it." After that season the left-hander went to the Arizona Instructional League. I worked with Shawn all winter, helping him focus on things he could control. Forget errors and bad umpire calls. Estes came to understand what Arthur Ashe said: "You are really never playing an opponent. You are playing yourself." Once Estes learned how to get out of his own way he became an All-Star with the San Francisco Giants.

A person's self-concept is vitally important. On his deathbed, Sigmund Freud said the essence of success in life is love and work. As individuals we all want to feel lovable and capable. If you don't feel good about yourself, you tend not to perform well. Those who have a negative self-image find ways to self-destruct. Darryl Strawberry is a prime example. Why would an athlete blessed with so much talent and given so many opportunities to succeed continually defeat himself with drug abuse?

In psychology there is something we call the self-consistency theory. It means we act consistent to our self-concept—our self-image. Throughout this book we will talk about the importance of seeing yourself as being successful. If you don't see yourself as successful, then your chances of succeeding are diminished. When good things happen, you tend to discount them.

We all have self-defeating thoughts and behaviors that undermine performance. I call them gremlins, the little invisible creatures that prevent athletes from performing at their best. Here's my gremlin checklist. If any one of them sounds familiar, you might want to turn to the section that deals with it specifically.

**Fear.** We all have a primitive fight-or-flight mechanism built into us to survive. It's a neurochemical response. We are ready to fight or flee whatever is threatening us. As we learned earlier, the body treats all vivid images as if they are real and happening now. In reality, most dangers are not a threat to life or limb. They are a psychological threat to self-esteem and ego. Why else would a brain surgeon turn to jelly over a four-foot downhill breaking putt? It's a threat to self-image. Fear actually can paralyze you.

**Anger.** We have to learn to control our emotions or they will control us. Anger is born out of frustration and expectations. Our minds and bodies don't always work together, as illustrated in a *Peanuts* cartoon. Lucy is holding the ball for Charlie Brown to kick. When he misses, Lucy tells him he has to use his mind and body. Charlie

Brown informs Lucy that his mind and body haven't talked to each other in years.

**Anxiety.** This is a generalized feeling of uncertainty or dread. A sense that something bad is going to happen. In baseball, some pitchers look great warming up on the side, but once they step across the chalk line and onto the field, they don't perform well. We call this "White Line Fever." We all become anxious, but people plagued by this gremlin get anxious about being anxious. This only leads to trouble.

**Self-consciousness.** Some athletes are afraid of looking bad or embarrassing themselves. They focus on the image of how they look instead of the task at hand. Ozzie Smith said, "Show me a guy who is afraid of looking bad and I can beat him every time." You can't perform well if you're afraid of embarrassing yourself.

**Perfectionism.** Shawn Estes was his own worst enemy because he never was satisfied with his performance. Self-critical, negative perfectionists can never do enough. Their mind-set often is fueled by a fear of failure. Perfectionists often have a very critical, self-condemning voice. I believe perfectionism often comes from conditional parenting. Many Little League parents don't realize the damage they do to their child's self-esteem with their negative comments. When you tell a Little Leaguer that he failed,

43

you're telling him that he *is* a failure. Children internalize criticism. Critical, condemning coaches who use fear and embarrassment injure a young person's psychological health.

**Stubbornness.** Some people are stubborn, unwilling to learn. They're not open to change. They believe the devil they know is better than the devil they don't know. They aren't going to take risks that will help them reach the next level. This is unfortunate because in sports you must learn how to fail successfully.

**Lack of motivation.** Some athletes simply lack the drive to become the best they can be. You can't buy motivation. You can't obtain it from someone else. "Motivation is something nobody else can give you," Joe DiMaggio said. "Others can help motivate you, but basically it must come from you, and it must be a constant desire to do your very best at all times and under any circumstances."

**Competitiveness.** We all are competitive. We all want to grow and succeed. But I think that early in life many people become discouraged as a result of negative experiences in sports. Some have coaches who embarrass them or play favorites. As a result those people become easily discouraged and develop an attitude that says, "What's the sense in trying?" This is learned helplessness. Others are lazy. They aren't willing to do the work. Every year I get calls from athletes who say "Mack, I should have listened to you." Many of them had plenty of natural talent but weren't willing to put in the time and work to reach their full potential. They thought they could get by on talent alone but later admit to themselves that they couldn't.

**Distractions.** Some athletes lead conflicting lifestyles. They aren't willing to discipline themselves. Strawberry, whose drug addiction has led to repeated suspensions, is a poster boy for this gremlin. Author Pete Gent, a former Dallas Cowboy, said, "Athletes hang around with people who tell them, 'The rules don't apply to you.'" The athlete who thinks he can party all night and still play the next day is subject to Newton's Law. What goes up must come down. In baseball, it's often his batting average that does.

**Persistence.** Remaining optimistic during difficult times isn't easy. But the most successful people are those who look at setbacks as opportunities for comebacks. They are persistent. They refuse to lose. Look at Jim Abbott: born without a right hand, he played ten years in the major leagues and threw a no-hitter. Look at Lance Armstrong: the American cyclist overcame cancer and won the Tour de France two years in a row. Look at Kurt Warner, who went from working in a grocery store to quarterbacking the St. Louis Rams to victory in the Super Bowl.

*It's important to look at yourself and identify your gremlins. In sports, as in life, the first step to success is getting out of your own way.*

# THE NEXT LEVEL

*It's what you learn after you know it all that counts.*

—EARL WEAVER

*Build your weaknesses until they become your strengths.*

—KNUTE ROCKNE

A few years ago I went to Japan and worked with a Japanese professional baseball team. It is one of my most memorable sports experiences. One thing I learned from my association with the Orix Blue Wave is a concept called *kaizen* which means constant daily learning and improvement. This concept is used not only in sports but also in businesses around the world, and it's wonderfully illustrated in a movie titled *Mr. Baseball*.

In the film Tom Selleck plays Jack Elliott, a veteran power-hitting first baseman for the New York Yankees. When Jack becomes mired in an extended hitting slump, the club replaces him in the lineup with a younger player. Elliott's agent sends Jack to Japan where he signs a lucrative contract.

When Elliott reports to his new club, the Dragons, he is an arrogant know-it-all. The former World Series MVP clashes with his Japanese manager, a rigid, no-nonsense disciplinarian. In America, it is said, you play baseball; in Japan, you *work* baseball.

On the first day of batting practice, Jack demonstrates his power, driving fastballs—his pitch—deep into the stands. The coach then instructs his pitcher to throw some off-speed stuff. The picture of confidence, Elliott swings and misses. He swings again, bruising nothing but the air. Through an interpreter, the manager informs his new player that he has "a hole in his swing."

In games, opposing pitchers don't offer Elliott fastballs. The frustrated American doesn't see any, either, until he admits he has a weakness and works toward patching the hole in his swing. By the end of the movie Jack Elliott, who came to Japan with a full teacup, thinking he knew it all, becomes a better hitter and more complete player. The Japanese teach the American humility. In turn, Jack teaches his manager and Japanese teammates how to have more fun playing the game.

Japanese players focus on the process of knowing themselves and improving their weaknesses. Americans seem more focused on outcome. At rookie camp I ask every player, whether he is Alex Rodriguez or Ken Griffey Jr., to train his thoughts on the process: What can I learn today? How can I become better tomorrow? Instead of worrying about statistics and outcomes, I want them thinking about the process of learning, growing, and getting better. Learning how to learn takes work.

"You never stop learning in this game," said Randy Johnson, ace of the Arizona Diamondbacks' pitching staff. "If you ever think you know everything about the game, it will jump up and bite you. Hard."

I believe in the Parachute Principle. The mind is like a parachute—it only works when it's open.

Athletes who hope to improve must *recognize* their strengths and weaknesses. Then they must work at turning their weaknesses into strengths. The great Hank Aaron, reflecting upon his early years in the major leagues, said, "I did a lot of thinking about hitting. I studied the pitchers all the time, and when I found one giving me trouble, I studied him extra hard. I wanted to know why he was getting me out and what I could do about it. Don Drysdale of the Dodgers used to get me out with a change-of-pace-pitch. In fact, all the Dodgers used to kill me with that pitch. So after my first year, when I got home to Mobile [Alabama], I got my brother Tommy to throw change-ups to me all the time. After that, they didn't throw me that pitch very often."

Magic Johnson's father taught his son the value of working on every phase of his game, especially the part that needed the most work. "Dad said my opponents would always find my weaknesses, and that it wouldn't take long, at any level, for them to start exploiting me," Johnson recalls. "He said my weaknesses would stand out like a neon sign. If I couldn't dribble with my left hand, or if I had the habit of being lazy on defense, everybody would know it. He told me that in basketball I couldn't hide."

Weekend golfers go to what they call the "driving" range, which actually is the practice range. Many spend 70 percent of their practice time seeing how far they can hit the ball even though as much as 70 percent of the game is played from 100 yards in.

It's human nature to practice the things we enjoy most and do well. "In truth," says golfer Nancy Lopez, "we should do just the opposite if we hope to improve." Pete Rose said it this way: "What's tough is to go out and work hard on the things that you don't do very well."

Tiger Woods reevaluated himself and his game after winning the Masters by a record margin in 1997. Recognizing his weaknesses, he made subtle changes in his swing and became more accurate and consistent off the tee. I played tournament tennis in high school and college. I had a weak backhand. When I was younger I could run around it, so I never worked on that weakness. Now that I can't run around it, my backhand is better than my forehand.

Most people resist making changes. They prefer to stay in a comfort zone. The paradox is that sometimes you have to get worse before you get better. It takes a leap of faith to make changes and work on weaknesses. What if Aaron hadn't gone back to Mobile and practiced hitting change-ups? Would he have become the hitter that he did? Probably not.

What do you do well? What don't you do so well? Where are the holes in your game? Be honest with yourself and open to learning. Be accepting of your weakness rather than resisting. Develop your own action plan to turn your shortcomings into strengths.

*Remember, your mind is like a parachute. It only works when it's open. What did you learn today and how will it make you better tomorrow? Work on your weaknesses until they become your strong points.*

# PART II

# LIVING THE DREAM

# GOOD ENOUGH
# TO DREAM

*You must have dreams and goals if you are ever going to achieve anything in this world.*

—LOU HOLTZ

*Be the dream.*

—JOHN CHANEY

On the evening of October 4, 1989, I couldn't get the grin off my face. I was in Chicago, my father's hometown, sitting in a box seat at a baseball park he loved. It was a rare and wondrous event for three reasons. First, the Cubs were in the playoffs. Second, this was the first ever post-season night game at Wrigley Field. The atmosphere was as electric as the wattage that illuminated the diamond, the outfield grass, the stands, and the ivy-covered wall. On that mild evening, with a hint of fall in the air, the old ballpark took on a magical glow.

But for me, the real magic was listening to the pregame introduction. I'll never forget the inner pleasure I felt when the public-address announcer's metallic voice crackled over the speakers. "Batting fifth, the left-fielder, Dwight Smith . . ."

As I sat there, beaming, my mind flashed to a day four years earlier. It all came back to me. The four walls. The funky furnishings. The single overhead bulb, as dim as the Wrigley klieg lights were bright.

I was back where this story begins—Mesa, Arizona. Room 106 of an economy motel.

Every major league team can judge a prospect's tools, and there are five in baseball—the ability to hit, hit with power, run, catch, and throw. But how do you measure what's inside an athlete's head and heart?

As the Cubs' new counselor, my job at spring training in 1985 was to interview about thirty of the club's young prospects. At our motel, I would telephone each one and ask him to come to my room.

They walked in, tentatively, one at a time, every thirty minutes. Barrio kids. Inner city kids. Country boys. California surfers. Youth on parade. Seated on a bed, I introduced myself with a smile and offered the chair across from me.

"Tell me," I asked for openers, "where do you see yourself in three or four years?" That's the usual timetable for a baseball player to make it to the major leagues. Some kids shrugged. They didn't see past tomorrow. Some hadn't thought that far ahead. Most didn't have a clear definition of where they wanted to be or what they wanted to do. Asked what motivated him, one young player said, candidly, "The Ford factory in Toledo." He knew he didn't want to be punching a time card there.

Then Dwight Smith strolled in. I can't remember for sure what he was wearing—T-shirt and shorts, I think— but I'll never forget his smile. Smitty's face lit the room. When I asked Dwight his vision for the future, the young man who wasn't a high-round draft choice didn't hesitate. "Mack, I see myself in Wrigley Field, hitting .300," he said. This kid from rural South Carolina pictured himself starting in the outfield. He even saw, and heard, himself singing the national anthem. Without prompting, Smitty suddenly broke into a Luther Vandross song. He had a good voice, and he knew it.

Dwight Smith saw his tomorrow in vivid color. As I listened, my skin broke out in goosebumps. I was struck by his confidence and moved by the power of his dream.

In 1989 Smitty made it to the big leagues. He celebrated his twenty-sixth birthday that year by finishing second to his Cubs roommate, Jerome Walton, as National League rookie of the year. Dwight was the only player nominated on all twenty-four ballots. He later sang "The Star-Spangled Banner" at Wrigley Field and at other major league parks as well. He ended his career in Atlanta where he sang the anthem before a Braves playoff game and earned a World Series ring.

The idea for this book came to me the day I flew to Chicago to watch Smitty play. During the flight I began putting down on paper what I had learned about the psychology of achievement and the psychology of success. Some people, I learned, are PSO—positive sensory oriented. Others are negative sensory oriented. Positive sensory oriented people, like Dwight Smith, have very vivid imaginations and sensory-rich dreams. Martin Luther King Jr. said, "I have a dream." He didn't say, "I have a good idea."

Wade Boggs, at age six, knew he someday would play in the major leagues. Johnny Bench's second-grade teacher asked her students what they wanted to be when they grew up. Bench said he wanted to be a baseball player. His classmates laughed. In the eighth grade he was asked the same question. "I said a ball player and they laughed a little more," Bench recalls. "By the eleventh grade, no one was laughing."

Michael Jordan said: "I think people like Julius Erving, Denzel Washington, Spike Lee, and Martin Luther King—people I admire—all created their own vision. And they didn't let anyone or anything distract them or break them down."

It is said that extraordinary people live their lives backward. They create a future, and then they live into it. An exercise I teach is called **A.C.T.** backward. I want you to try it. The **A** stands for accept your present state. Understand your strengths and weaknesses, as we discussed in the last section. **C** stands for create your desired state. Dwight Smith had a dream. What's your dream? Close your eyes, and see yourself exactly the way you want to be. Write down what this desired state would look like. **T** stands for take action steps to get you there. Success is a journey of one step at a time. And the longest journey begins with the first step.

*Believe in the power of your dream, then **A.C.T.** backward. Accept your present state. Create your desired state. Take action through goal setting.*

# Progress Not Perfection

*I'm a firm believer in goal setting. Step by step. I can't see any other way of accomplishing anything.*
—Michael Jordan

*It's all about the journey, not the outcome.*
—Carl Lewis

Two university researchers spent years studying thousands of peak performers in industries of all kinds, including sports. What Edwin Locke and Gary Latham discovered is that people who succeed are goal oriented. They have a vision. They create sensory-rich dreams like those illustrated in the last section. Then they turn that vision into action through goal setting.

Goal setting is a master skill for personal growth and peak performance. I can't stress this too much. Without goals, where will you go in life? If you don't know where you are headed, you're probably going to wind up somewhere other than where you want to be.

Dick Hannula, one of the most successful high school swimming coaches in the country, said, "Motivation depends in a very large part on goal setting. The coach must have goals. The team must have goals. Each individual swimmer must have goals—real, vivid, living goals. . . . Goals keep everyone on target."

Goal setting is a way of bringing the future into the present so you can take action now. Goals improve performance. Goals improve the quality of practices. They clarify expectations and help increase self-confidence by seeing yourself get better. As the swimming coach points out, goals also increase the motivation to achieve.

Let's look at some basic principles of goal setting. First, you should develop performance goals as well as outcome goals. A performance goal, or action goal, is something you can control. If you play baseball and you want to hit .300, then you are going to have to take a certain number of pitches in batting practice. I ask major league hitters to concentrate on having four quality at-bats each game. That becomes their goal rather than "I'm going to get two hits every game." Focusing on quality at-bats is an action goal. The outcome will take care of itself.

Goals should be challenging but realistic. "Setting goals for your game is an art," golfer Greg Norman said. "The trick is in setting them at the right level, neither too low nor too high. A good goal should be lofty enough to inspire hard work, yet realistic enough to provide solid hope of attainment." Dick Hannula put it this way: "Goals must be high enough to excite you, yet not so high that you cannot vividly imagine them. Goals must be attainable, but just out of reach for now."

An acronym for setting goals is **SMART**. The **S** stands for specific. Say you want to make the Little League or high school team as a third baseman. A specific goal would be to work on your fielding skills. **M** is for measurable. "Every day I'm going to take one hundred ground balls to my left." The **A** stands for achievable. The goal is reachable and within your control. **R** is for realistic. It's believable. **T** stands for time-bound. There is an accomplishment date. A goal is a dream with a time line. Every goal needs a target date for completion.

I encourage athletes to set daily or short-term goals. The way to achieve long-term goals is to break them down into small steps. Effective goal setting is like a staircase. Each step is an action step—an increment of progress. The old saying is "Inch by inch it's a cinch."

One day I received a telephone call from the general manager of an NFL team. With concern in his voice, he said the club's young quarterback, a first-round draft pick, wasn't sleeping well. At night, he began drinking alcohol to help him sleep, which only created other problems. So I met with the player and the team executive and we agreed to work together for a specific period of time. I was establishing a goal right there.

At our first session, the player was very open with me. He talked about his five-year contract and the size of his salary. The club expected him to take over the offense and lead his teammates to the playoffs. Management, coaches, and fans were counting on him. The responsibility felt overwhelming.

The rookie had the gottas. "I gotta do this . . . I gotta do that." He was thinking about accomplishing everything at once. He worried about the future, which he had no control over. Together, we devised a five-year road map and marked it with a series of small but significant steps for him to follow. We set short-term goals. Specific goals. SMART goals.

After our meeting, the rookie seemed like a different person. He felt empowered. He had a can-do action plan and therefore felt more in control. Two of our greatest fears are the fear of being out of control and the fear of the unknown. Setting and attaining small goals provided the player with positive feedback and the motivation to get better. As he improved, his confidence grew.

When he still was in Class A ball, a young Diamondbacks pitcher called my 1-800 hotline. He was in a panic. When I asked his problem, the major-league prospect said he had started the season strong, winning four of five games. Since then he had lost three in a row. He sounded more than disappointed. This kid had never had a losing record in his life and now was questioning his future in professional baseball.

I began to quiz him. What was his earned run average during the three losses compared with the start of the season? His ERA was lower, he said. How about your first pitches? He said he was throwing more strikes. I told him that despite what he thought, he was improving. The outcomes just weren't going his way. I helped him understand that he has no control over his record. What he can control is his ERA, his walks-per-strikeout ratio, and his hits allowed per inning. He didn't have to be perfect. Seek progress, not perfection, I told him.

What do you want to accomplish in sports? The magic begins when you set goals. What are your goals? Make a list. Write them down. This is the first step to putting your dreams into action and turning them into a reality.

*Goals are dreams with time lines. Turn your vision into action with goal setting. Seek progress rather than perfection.*

# DON'T SHIRK THE WORK

*Talent is never enough. With few exceptions the best players are the hardest workers.*
—MAGIC JOHNSON

*The harder you work the harder it is to surrender.*
—VINCE LOMBARDI

For six years I spent my summers in the mountains of Flagstaff, training-camp home of the NFL Cardinals. At seven thousand feet, breathing in the clean pine-scented air, players began the task of preparing themselves physically and mentally for the grind of the upcoming season. Under the bright July sun, rookies hoping to make the team and veterans battling to keep their jobs ran sprints, or gassers. They put on pads and banged heads in practice twice a day.

We all *want* to win. Every athlete *wants* to succeed. But the ones who do are those who separate wanting from being willing to make the sacrifice that winning demands. After the first few days of practice, at high altitude, I could look into players' eyes, observe their body language, and tell which ones were determined to pay the price to make their dreams come true. One of those players was Ricky Proehl.

I met Ricky in 1990 after his senior season at Wake Forest. He attended the NFL scouting combine in Indianapolis. At the combine, hundreds of pro prospects are interviewed, weighed, measured, timed, examined, and evaluated in advance of the league's spring draft. As the Cardinals' team counselor, I interviewed dozens of players. I liked Ricky Proehl immediately. This cocky wideout from New Jersey didn't fit the NFL prototype. Most scouts thought he was undersized and probably not fast enough to compete against the pro game's hiccup-quick cornerbacks and safeties. But I liked his attitude, and I admired his confidence.

Proehl had led Wake Forest in receiving three years in a row. He set the school record for career receptions. He saw himself playing in the NFL, just as a young Dwight Smith saw himself wearing a Cubs uniform in Wrigley Field. Other prospects who had competed against Proehl in the Atlantic Coast Conference offered testimonials to his work ethic: "Ricky Proehl? He comes at you, play after play." "He runs perfect routes." "The guy's a fighter. He never quits." I hoped the Cardinals would draft him, and they did in the third round.

Ten years later, late in the fourth quarter of the NFC championship game, the St. Louis Rams broke from the huddle. They trailed Tampa Bay, 6–5, a baseball score.

Less than five minutes remained. Kurt Warner, the Rams' quarterback, called the play: Flex Left Smoke Right 585 H-Choice. At the snap the team's fourth receiver took off down the left sideline. He looked up into the dome lights, eyes widening. Here it came, a tight spiral. The receiver fended off a defender with his right arm and caught the ball with his left.

Touchdown. That thirty-yard catch won the game and sent the Rams to the Super Bowl and put number eighty-seven—Ricky Proehl—on the cover of *Sports Illustrated*. "This is what I dreamed about playing in the NFL for ten years," Proehl said that day. The kid from Wake Forest, traded by the Cardinals to a losing team in Seattle and then to a bad team in Chicago and later to a 4–12 team in St. Louis, took a lap around the Trans World Dome, clutching the George Halas NFC championship trophy.

Lars Anders at the University of Florida, writing in a paper on "Deliberate Practice," said he found it takes ten years of practice to acquire the mastery of an expert. Ricky Proehl has been catching footballs for a long time, but it took him ten years of hard work to become an overnight success.

In sports, as in life, there is no substitute for commitment. Vince Lombardi called it heart power. "A man can be as great as he wants to be," the Hall of Fame coach said. "If you believe in yourself and have the courage, the determination, the dedication, the competitive drive, and if you are willing to sacrifice the little things in life and pay the price for the things that are worthwhile, it can be done. Once a man has made a commitment . . . he puts the greatest strength in the world behind him. It's something we call heart power. Once a man has made this commitment, nothing will stop him short of success."

Listen to Tony Gwynn, one of baseball's best hitters: "It's easy to cheat yourself and do just enough to get by, but that's what everybody can do, just enough to get by. But those who want to be successful and maintain that level of success have got to push a little bit harder and do a little bit more."

Rod Carew says he has seen many baseball players blessed with God-given ability who simply didn't want to work. "They are soon gone," Carew says. "I've seen others with no ability to speak of who stayed in the big leagues for fourteen or fifteen years. . . . You have to *want* to do the work."

Andre Agassi fell from the top of the tennis world to number 141 in the rankings. Determined to resurrect his career, he committed to the belief that if he worked himself into top physical shape no one could beat him. "You have to work hard and establish yourself all over again or else it's real easy to have a bad day," Agassi said. Watching him during his inspiring comeback, you could see Agassi was willing to stay out on the court for as long as he had to to beat his chief rival, Pete Sampras.

Rob Evans transformed the Ole Miss basketball program into a powerhouse. This is what Evans, now head coach at Arizona State, tells his players: "Hey, you might not be as good as Michael Jordan, but there isn't any reason you can't play with as much effort and enthusiasm as he does. No matter where you are talent-wise, you always can play hard."

How about you? Have you made a commitment to this book? Reading the lessons for enjoyment is fine. But results come only after you cross that line and say you're going to answer the questions and do the exercises. Mental skills, like physical skills, only improve if you do the work.

One of my favorite quotes is from former tennis great Bjorn Borg. "I remember how I used to take the train to Stockholm every day after school to play, coming home late, studying, getting up to go to school, getting on the train again, all those years. It has gotten results. But even if it hadn't, even if I wasn't able to become a champion, I would still know that I gave it my best shot. I tried. I got on the train and I tried."

Have you boarded the train? Are you on track? If not, what are you waiting for?

*It takes years of hard work to become an overnight success. Are you willing to make the commitment and pay the price?*

# Fatal Distractions

*Obstacles are what you see when you take your eyes off your goal.*
—Jim Lefebvre

*In spite of all the distractions, remain focused on the job.*
—Reggie Jackson

His name means "almost there" in Navajo. And by the end of Notah Begay's rookie year on the PGA Tour, the golf world agreed that he had arrived. Begay, a full-blooded Native American, won two tournaments in 1999. The young man who played college golf with Tiger Woods at Stanford and earned a degree in economics became a hero and a source of inspiration to his people.

But two months after his hometown of Albuquerque, New Mexico, honored him with Notah Begay Day, the twenty-seven-year-old made embarrassing headlines when he was arrested and convicted on a drunk-driving charge. After Begay told a New Mexico judge about a prior drunk-driving offense in Arizona, he received a seven-day jail term. He was also fined and ordered to perform community service.

To his credit, Begay put the blame squarely where it belonged. "You're looking at someone who is going to jail," Begay told a group of kids attending a junior clinic. "I would hate to see you go through what I have to. But I made a bad decision and I am taking responsibility for that."

Not long ago, I received a call from ESPN Sports. A Phoenix radio affiliate wanted to interview me, not about the mental game and athletic excellence but rather about all the trouble we see in the sports arena. Every day the sports pages print embarrassing and tragic headlines: drug suspensions, domestic violence, paternity suits, crimes involving weapons, drunken driving charges, car crashes, fatalities. Having served as a counselor for several professional sports teams, I know athletes and other individuals whose careers and lives have been damaged by the bad choices and mistakes they have made.

Lynn Larson earned a Super Bowl ring while playing with the old Baltimore Colts. Lynn and I once gave talks together about leadership in sports. We discussed what he calls fatal distractions. As we talked about in the previous section on goal setting, whatever your age and whatever your game, you need to focus your time and energy if you want to become successful and realize your dreams. One key to reaching your full potential as a person and an athlete is to avoid those distractions that can lead you away from your goals.

Satchel Paige, the legendary pitcher and philosopher, once said, "Go very light on the vices, such as carrying on in society. The social ramble ain't restful." Satchel took his own advice, which is still valid today.

I spend every Thanksgiving weekend speaking to hundreds of young people at the Griffey International baseball camp at Disney World in Orlando. One thing I do during the camp always gets quite a reaction. I have this fake snake. It looks very realistic. It hisses and even coils around your arm. Standing before the group, I'll reach into a cloth sack and pull out the snake and hold it up for all to see. The kids scatter.

"Next time someone brings drugs to your school yard I want you to do the same thing," I tell them. "Drugs are just as poisonous as this snake."

Say yes to sports and no to drugs, nicotine, and supplements. Carl Lewis, the six-time Olympic gold medalist, says there are three things to remember about drugs. "The first is that if you take drugs, you'll never know your full potential. Second, there is the obvious health risk. And third, if you do drugs, you're quitting on yourself."

I admire Joe Garagiola. The broadcaster and former big-league catcher is leading the campaign against smokeless tobacco. Garagiola's good friend, Bill Tuttle, developed cancer of the mouth after chewing tobacco for years. Brett Butler, a tobacco user, had a cancerous tumor removed from his throat. Joe talks to major-league players in an effort to get them to consider the effects of tobacco on their health as well as the potential impact the habit can have on kids.

Supplements of all kinds are readily available. During the 1999–2000 NBA season, Phoenix Suns forward Tom Gugliotta took a dietary supplement which he said was given to him by an old high school friend to help him sleep. Seated on the team bus after a game in Portland, Gugliotta suffered a seizure that temporarily caused him to stop breathing. He was hospitalized and connected to a respirator. "I took something I really didn't know too much about," Gugliotta said. "That's not right to do, and it almost cost me my life."

Follow your goals and not the crowd. Former Olympic swimming champion Janet Evans said, "Sometimes I feel envious when my friends go to parties, and I have to go to bed. But my friends always tell me that the parties really aren't that much fun anyway. Whatever I've missed, I've made up for. Most kids don't get to go to the Olympics and win three gold medals. It's definitely been worth it."

As a teenager, basketball star Kevin Johnson went to the gym every evening to practice. One evening the janitor said to him, "Kevin, it's Saturday night. Why aren't you out at parties, like everybody else?"

"Parties," Johnson replied, "won't take me where I want to go."

Don't do anything to embarrass yourself, your family, or the team. Joe Gibbs preached this when he coached the Washington Redskins teams that played in the Super Bowl. Joe Bugel, a former Gibbs assistant, made it his number one rule when he became head coach of the Arizona Cardinals.

Associate with people who will make you better. Richard Dumas, a promising talent with the Phoenix Suns, battled drug problems. He got into trouble during the off-season when he returned home to Tulsa and fell into the company of old friends. Sometimes you have to let go of old friendships in order to stay on track to reach your goals.

Be big enough to back away from trouble. Many athletes become targets. Branch Rickey told the great Jackie Robinson that he didn't want someone who was big enough to handle trouble. He wanted someone who was big enough to walk away from it. Today, some athletes arm themselves with handguns. In my opinion, nothing good comes from carrying a weapon.

Don't abuse alcohol. Golfer John Daly is only one example of a gifted athlete whose personal and professional life has been torn apart by alcohol. Drinking ruined more than one marriage and cost Daly millions in endorsement contracts. "I know now," said Dwight Gooden, a former Cy Young Award winner, "that it was drinking that destroyed my fastball." Drinking and driving cost a promising young player with the Arizona Diamondbacks his life. If you are of legal age and drink alcohol, follow Knute Rockne's rule: Drink the first, sip the second, and refuse the third.

Take responsibility for your life and your actions. Too many successful athletes don't think the rules of society apply to them.

*What you find depends upon where you look. Stay focused on your goals and avoid the fatal distractions. Say yes to your dreams and no to drugs.*

# FATE LOVES
# THE FEARLESS

*Really it comes down to your philosophy. Do you want to
play it safe and be good or do you want to take a chance and
be great?*

—JIMMY JOHNSON

*The bottom line is you can't be afraid to fail.*

—JERRY COLANGELO

There is a saying in baseball that you can't steal second
with your feet on first. Whenever I hear that maxim I
picture Rickey Henderson edging off the first-base bag,
taking his lead and then extending it, stealthily, little by
little, his watchful eyes fixed on the pitcher, larceny in his
heart. Would Henderson have stolen more bases than any
player in major league history if he were afraid to risk
being thrown out? How about Babe Ruth? Would he
have hit 714 home runs if he feared striking out, which
he did 1,330 times?

The answer, obviously, is no. And yet the fear of failure, more than any single thing, keeps people in sports,
and in all avenues of life, from realizing their full poten-

tial. Fear of failure prevents more of us from succeeding than any opponent. Fear creates the conditions that keep athletes from winning.

"Fear of failure can restrict a player," said Chuck Noll, the former Pittsburgh Steelers coach. "It can kill him as an individual. If one continually worries about failing, he'll get so tight that he will fail."

One of the paradoxes of sports is that fear of failure actually makes failure more likely. As Noll said, the thought of negative consequences threatens you, inhibits you, and tightens you up. Fear of failure leads to contracted muscles and shortened breathing. It overloads the system with stress. Fear makes you play safe. Fear makes you play small.

Here's an interesting experiment. Take someone with a strong fear of failure. Give the person several wadded sheets of paper and ask him or her to toss them into a wastebasket from three different spots—directly over the basket, from fifteen feet away, and from forty feet away. Studies have shown that those who fear failure will feel most anxious from fifteen feet. Standing over the basket they know success is guaranteed. From forty feet away they have no expectations to succeed. From fifteen feet they feel they should be able to toss the paper ball into the basket, but they know there is a chance they may fail.

You also see this in golf. Facing an impossible forty-foot putt, a golfer is more relaxed than when he stands over a dreaded four-footer. Why? Because the player is afraid to fail. When you're not afraid to fail, your chances of succeeding improve.

Where does this fear come from? Oftentimes behind the fear of failure is perfectionism. I think perfectionism is reinforced in society. In school, from an early age, we are told what we got wrong on a test instead of what we got right. When I was in graduate school I told my counselor I was a perfectionist. "Oh, yeah," the counselor replied. "Tell me, Gary, what are you perfect at?"

Do you know how gemologists tell a fake emerald from a real one? The fakes are perfect. Real emeralds have flaws. None of us is perfect.

Oftentimes, beneath the desire to succeed and achieve excellence is an ultra-critical, demanding, and judgmental voice. This internal voice beats the person up, mentally and emotionally. We learned this from pitcher Shawn Estes, who realized he was an impatient perfectionist. When Rick Wolff worked with the Cleveland Indians he wrote an article about the perfect-pitch syndrome. An example of this condition is a successful Triple A pitcher who is called up to the major leagues. Instead of trusting his stuff, the pitcher thinks he has to be perfect against big-league hitting. So he tries to nibble on the corners of the plate. Because he is new to the big show, umpires don't give him the close pitches. The harder the pitcher tries to paint the corners the farther behind in the count he falls. The more he gets behind in the count, the greater the hitter's advantage becomes. When the first pitch is a strike, the major league batting average is below .200. If the first pitch is a ball, the batting average jumps to more than .300.

Procrastination is a part of perfectionism in some people. Those who procrastinate don't do anything. By not doing anything, they can't fail. It's an inhibiting, self-defeating cycle.

Fear keeps people from taking risks. And sometimes the greatest risk is not to take a risk. If Jerry Colangelo were afraid of failure, one of sport's most successful businessmen might not have left the Hungry Hill neighborhood of Chicago where he grew up, or played basketball at the University of Illinois, or moved to the desert southwest to run the new NBA team, the Phoenix Suns. If Colangelo hadn't been willing to take a risk, there wouldn't be an America West Arena in downtown Phoenix, and Arizona might not have a major league baseball team.

Tennis great Billie Jean King made a profound statement about failure. She said athletes should look at failure as feedback. All-Star pitcher Greg Maddux put it another way: "Failure is the best teacher in the world. . . . You get to learn from what happens to you—both good and bad—in a real-live game situation. I've given up a lot of runs in my career, and that means I've made a lot of mistakes, and I've had to learn from them. . . . The hitters have a funny way of telling you that a particular pitch isn't working."

Failing to learn is learning to fail. By looking at failure as feedback you can change how you feel.

Michael Jordan calls fear an illusion. He and many other great athletes learn to turn fear into anger. You can run from fear, or you can get angry and attack it. If you challenged Jordan's pride he wouldn't be afraid. He used that energy to become more aggressive. Good athletes take fear of failure and turn it around.

Look at fear as a natural part of growing and learning. People who succeed aren't afraid to fail. Failure can be a better teacher than winning.

*Learn how to fail successfully. Hate to fail but never fear it. Learn to view failure as feedback.*

# PERMISSION TO WIN

*You can't outperform your self-image.*
—DENNIS CONNOR

*Life is a collection of self-fulfilling prophecies.*
—JOHN NABOR

Before the tournament began, few gave him a chance to contend, much less win. Jean Van de Velde was a 150-to-1 underdog. But to the amazement of the golf world, and Scottish bookmakers, there he was on Sunday, standing on the tee of the 72nd hole at Carnoustie, leading the 1999 British Open by three shots.

One hole to go. All Van de Velde had to do was make six at number 18. A double bogey and golf's oldest prize was his. The soft voice of reason told the dashing Frenchman to do the smart thing: play conservatively. Hit a five iron off the tee, then another five iron, then a wedge to the green. Two putts later and Van de Velde could kiss his wife and lift the claret jug in celebration as the first Frenchman to win a major golf championship in ninety-two years.

But Van de Velde didn't play it safe. In the gathering gloom, a light rain falling, he hit his driver. The ball sailed wildly off line. Instead of wedging his next shot back onto the fairway, Van de Velde took a full swing with a two-iron. The ball bounced off the grandstands and disappeared into the rough. His next shot was from a terrible lie and landed in the winding creek that fronts the green. The world cringed as it watched him single-handedly turn the Open into a stage play as compelling and wrenching as *Les Miserables*.

Van de Velde didn't make six. He made seven and then lost in a playoff. When the nightmare was over, witnesses asked the same head-shaking question. Jean, why didn't you play it safe? Why hit a two-iron? The runner-up gave a little shrug. "Next time, I hit zee wedge," Van de Velde said, pasting on a brave smile. "You'll say I'm a coward, but I'll hit zee wedge."

Why didn't he? Because that's not the way Van de Velde saw himself. Even though a timid shot might have assured him victory, he played the hole boldly and fearlessly. "He *had* to play that way," his wife, Brigitte, said. "He had played that way all week." Van de Velde was being true to his self-image.

The golfer's collapse made one Scottish bookmaker look like a prophet. "The lead doesn't matter," he said before Van de Velde's final round. The bookie tapped the side of his head with a finger. The gesture seemed to suggest he had little faith the leader would hold up under the pressure. Van de Velde, who had won only one tournament on the European Tour, was out of his comfort zone.

There is a psychological principle called cognitive dissonance. It can be defined as the uncomfortable psychological state that arises when how you see yourself and what is really happening come into conflict. Many athletes who experience this conflict revert to their comfort zone.

"We all have an interior comfort zone that we want to be in," said Dennis Connor, the America's Cup skipper. "Picture a good club golfer playing Jack Nicklaus. His self-image is probably that he is a good golfer, but not good enough to beat Nicklaus. If he beat Nicklaus, he would be uncomfortable with the demands of his new self-image. So he does whatever he can to get back in that comfort zone, even if it means missing a two-foot putt on the 18th green."

Annika Sorenstam is a case in point. In an interview, the LPGA champion said that early in her career she was afraid of having to speak in public and felt so uncomfortable being the center of attention that she would deliberately miss putts on the later holes in tournaments just so she could finish second. She had a fear of success, which is fear of failure at the next level.

I love golf. I learned to play when I moved to Arizona. One day I was at my home course, on the 11th or 12th hole when a partner told me, "Gary, you know you're shooting even par?" I'm a ten handicapper. My image of myself is not that of a par golfer. As soon as I heard the words—"You're shooting par"—I felt such a pressure on myself that I pushed my next tee shot out of bounds. Triple bogey. After that, I relaxed again. I was back in my comfort zone.

There are a lot of comfort-zone athletes. I see many of them in Triple A baseball. During the last off-season I worked with a pitcher who has one of the liveliest arms in the game. In Triple A he is a dominating force. But every time he is placed in a major-league situation he falls apart. He can't see himself getting major leaguers out.

The Arizona Cardinals once drafted a wonderfully gifted running back. He was as big and strong as any back in the NFL. But he couldn't see himself as a starter. He couldn't even imagine himself being successful. His self-image wouldn't let him, therefore he wasn't in professional football for long.

Limits begin where vision ends. You have to see yourself as a no-limits person. For years, breaking the four-minute mile was thought to be physically impossible. Then in 1954 Roger Bannister ran the mile in 3:59.4. Over the next two years, fifty other runners broke the barrier. Why? They had an image. In Bannister they had a model for success.

Dennis Eckersley saw himself as a starting pitcher. Only when he reinvented his self-image and saw himself as a closer did he become a premier reliever. Recently retired Cubs' announcer Steve Stone, a former major league pitcher, talks about reprogramming your subconscious mind. "It's like wiping a blackboard clean and starting over," Stone said. "The spring before I won the Cy Young Award, I had to sit down and convince myself that I was better than a .500 pitcher."

Humans are the only species that get in the way of their own growth. The most important thing a parent can give a child is a positive self-image. People asked Spud Webb, who is five-foot-four, how in the world he thought he could play in the NBA. How did Jim Abbott expect to play baseball—much less pitch in the major leagues—with one arm? How would he field the ball? Olympic gold medal winner Wilma Rudolph said she had to overcome a lot of fears and self-images to become a success. Her first challenge was to learn to walk without leg braces.

Most of the work I do is as a "stretch" and not a "shrink." I help athletes expand their comfort zone and encourage them to take risks. If you don't see yourself succeeding, or you don't feel deserving, you will sabotage yourself.

Be willing to take a risk. Remember, there is no security in life. There is only adventure.

*Limits begin where vision ends. Visualize success and give yourself permission to win.*

# THE FIRE INSIDE

*Each of us has a fire in our hearts for something. It's our goal in life to find it and keep it lit.*

— MARY LOU RETTON

*All I want out of life is that when I walk down the street folks will say, "There goes the greatest hitter who ever lived."*

— TED WILLIAMS

He remembers gazing into the night sky as a boy, long, long ago. Each time he saw a falling star he made a wish. "Please," he said, "let me be the hitter I want to be." As he grew older, his love for hitting a baseball didn't fade as many childhood infatuations do. The art form became his focus, his passion, his singular goal. "A man has to have goals, for a day, for a lifetime," he said upon reflection. "Mine was to have people say, 'There goes Ted Williams, the greatest hitter who ever lived.'"

On July 13, 1999, major league baseball staged its annual midsummer classic at Fenway Park in Boston. It was a glorious evening, perfect for stargazing. As part of the pregame festivities, the National and American League All-Star teams were introduced to the sellout crowd. So were the legends of the game. One by one, the announcer presented the members of baseball's All-Century team.

Near the end of the roll call, a golf cart appeared in the old ballpark. Along with millions of other TV viewers, I watched as it slowly paraded around the field, its heroic passenger smiling, waving, greeted with warm cheers.

Cameras flashed like winking stars, and when the announcer welcomed him and honored him, his voice was close to reverence. "That's Ted Williams! The greatest hitter who ever lived."

Motivation is a popular word, especially in sports. It comes from a Latin word meaning "to move." Athletes can move in one of two ways, either toward seeking pleasure (rewards) or toward avoiding pain (punishment). Motivation can be the desire to succeed or the fear of failure. I believe the best and healthiest motivation is the one that pushed Ted Williams, the last major leaguer to hit over .400 in one season, to reach his goal and live his dream.

An athlete's success is said to depend upon four factors—physical ability, physical training, mental training, and desire or drive. The desire to succeed needs to be stronger than the fear of failure.

"You hear a lot of athletes who say they are motivated by a fear of failure," pitcher David Cone said. "I couldn't disagree more. To me, it's an opportunity. This is what we live and play for. There's no place I'd rather be than right here, right now, pitching big games down the stretch for the Yankees."

Muhammad Ali illustrates one of my favorite stories about motivation. When he was growing up in Louisville, he got a job sacking groceries. He didn't make much money, but he saved enough to buy a secondhand bicycle. He loved that blue bicycle. He was proud of it. He had worked hard for it and earned it. One day someone stole his bike. He was heartbroken.

"I walked all over Louisville that summer, looking for that bicycle," Ali said, picking up the narrative. "I walked and looked, looked and walked. Never found it to this day. But every time I got into the ring, I looked across at the other fighter and I told myself, 'Hey, *that's* the guy who stole my bicycle!'"

Athletes find motivation in different ways. Roger Clemens said he thrived on the doubts that others had of him. The pitcher went into the 1997 season intent on proving the Red Sox had made a mistake by letting him go.

The most successful athletes are self-motivated. "The most important thing is to love your sport," said Peggy Fleming, the former Olympic figure-skating champion. "Never do it to please someone else—it has to be yours. That is all that will justify the hard work needed to achieve success."

At a workshop with elite teenage athletes I asked one young man to relate his most enjoyable sports experience. He recalled being ten or eleven years old. He talked about how much fun he had shooting hoops. As the teen relived the memory, his father's eyes welled with tears. The young man who wanted to quit his high school team was still playing basketball for his father's sake. It was his dad's dream, not his own.

What we associate with pleasure we pursue. What we associate with pain we avoid. Playing sports as a kid should be an enjoyable, positive, and rewarding experience. But too often, impressionable youngsters are embarrassed by a coach, or they worry about pleasing their parents. Participating in sports then becomes a painful, even punishing experience. As a coach I would want my kids to have fun. I would want them to be eager and excited. I would want them to feel they are improving and focusing on the process rather than the outcome.

Motivation gets you moving in a direction. Being on a mission provides the emotion. Clemens was on a mission after he left the Red Sox. Arnold Schwarzenegger also had a mission. His vision created what he calls "want power." Schwarzenegger said, "My wanting to be Mr. Universe came about because I saw myself so clearly, being up there on the stage and winning."

Carl Lewis had an ambitious mission and a powerful vision, too. "I want to be remembered as a person who felt there was no limitation to what the human body and mind can do, and be the inspiration to lead people, and do things they never hoped to do."

At spring training, Alex Rodriguez designed T-shirts for himself and his Seattle Mariners teammates. The printed message read: "We're On A Mission, Sir."

How about you? Does a fire burn inside you? Do you have a mission? What is it? What motivates you? If it is fear of failure, let that emotion go. The best motivation is "want" power, that prideful desire to achieve.

*Find your passion and make it happen. Be on a mission and live your life on purpose. Be motivated by your desire to achieve rather than your fear of failure.*

# THE FOUR D'S

*Motivation gets you going. Discipline keeps you going.*
—JIM RYAN

*The only discipline that lasts is self-discipline.*
—BUM PHILLIPS

Several years ago, a Phoenix-area school district conducted a survey of its high school athletes. The results confirmed growing rumors and suspicions. Of the students at three high schools who responded to the survey, more than 20 percent said they knew teammates or other athletes who were using steroids.

The Paradise Valley district took quick action. Believing schools have an obligation to safeguard against the danger of drugs, the district instituted random drug testing of its high school athletes. The program made national news and sparked lively debate.

Some people outside the district told administrators that drug testing might put district athletes at a competitive disadvantage. "They think because other schools use steroids our athletes won't be able to compete without using them, too," said Toby Spessard, a district administrator. "That logic is strange, to say the least. If our athletes have healthy minds and bodies, and know they're going to compete fairly, I think that's an enormous advantage for us."

At the time, I was team counselor for the NFL Cardinals. The school district asked if I would sit on a committee and develop a program to educate coaches and athletes about drugs and offer strategies to improve performance without the use of drugs, especially steroids.

A sports medicine physician with the U.S. Olympic Committee conducted a study in which he asked young athletes this question: If a drug existed that would help you win an Olympic gold medal, but using it would take five years off your life, would you take it? More than half answered yes.

Learning how to use one's mind can be as potent as any performance-enhancing drug. In medical studies, many patients report improvement in their physical condition after they are given placebos, or sugar pills. Why? The power of the mind.

I developed a mental skills training program for drug-free athletes called "The Naturals." The night I outlined the program at a meeting with hundreds of high school athletes and their parents I brought along two Cardinals players, Garth Jax and Ron Wolfley.

Someone said that people who have no fear either are in mental institutions or on special teams. Wolfley played on special teams for the Cardinals. He made All-Pro running kamikaze missions, bolting downfield on punts and kickoffs, crashing full speed into oncoming opponents at great risk to his health and safety. As a player he was fearless and tough and the most quotable player in the locker room.

When I introduced Wolfley to the crowd, his message carried the same energy and passion with which he played the game. Ron spoke of a former NFL player he knew who took steroids and had become gravely ill. "I've seen steroids, and I'm telling you, I don't use any of that stuff," Wolfley proclaimed. "The only drugs I use are the four D's," and he ticked them off, one by one, his rising voice whip-cracking over the silent auditorium. "Desire . . . Dedication . . . Determination . . . Discipline. *Those* are the drugs I use! And I don't have to buy them on the street corner. They don't cost me anything." He pointed to his chest, to his heart. "I've got 'em right here."

**Desire.** We talked at great length about desire in the last section. "Want" power is as important as will power when it comes to accomplishing your goals. What's your wish? What do you long for? Ted Williams found his singular desire at an early age. What's your dream? How badly do you want it?

**Dedication.** Dedication is turning desire into action, which requires lasting commitment. Football coach Lou

Holtz said, "If you don't make a total commitment to whatever you are doing, then you start looking to bail out the first time the boat starts leaking." Randy Johnson, the most dominating power pitcher of our time, says the most tragic event in his life—his father died on Christmas Day, 1992—proved to be the turning point of his career. "That was the year my heart became a lot bigger," Johnson said. "It's a matter of maturity and it's a matter of my heart getting bigger and it's a matter of dedicating myself to be the best."

**Determination.** Everyone *wants* to be successful, but those who achieve success are steeled by an unwavering resolve. They are self-motivated—the kind of motivation that fueled and sustained Jack Nicklaus early in his pro career as he beat golf balls for an hour, then another, on the practice range until it was almost dark.

"Let's go, Jack," his new wife, Barbara, called out impatiently. "I'm hungry." With callused hands, Nicklaus hit another ball, then another, then another into the dying light. "So am I," Jack replied.

**Discipline.** It means doing what you have to do when you need to do it, whether you want to or not. Self-discipline—the only kind that lasts—is action oriented. It doesn't procrastinate, and it doesn't make excuses. "Setting a goal is not the main thing," said Tom Landry, the former Dallas Cowboys coach who is enshrined in the

Pro Football Hall of Fame. "It's deciding how you will go about achieving it and staying with that plan. The key is discipline."

*Once you have your dream and direction, it is desire, dedication, determination, and discipline that keep you going. Ask yourself this: Are you walking your talk?*

# PART III

# MIND-SET FOR SUCCESS

# Attitude Is Everything

*I firmly believe that the only disability in life is a bad attitude.*
—Scott Hamilton

*A bad attitude is worse than a bad swing.*
—Payne Stewart


Attitude is like a pair of eyeglasses. It is the lens through which we view the world. Positive-minded people see life around them through rose-tinted or clear glasses, while those who are negative squint through glasses that are dark and gloomy. Both types of people can look at the same event or situation and see it in two different lights.

Attitudes influence how we act and feel. They also affect performance. Former major leaguer Dave Winfield said, "So many players enter the game with the same approximate skills. The difference is not aptitude but attitude." Your attitude more than your aptitude determines your altitude—how high you go, how far you climb the ladder of success.

Optimists have a positive expectancy that helps them achieve their goals. Theirs is a can-do attitude. They take action, which is empowering. Pessimists take a passive attitude. They play the blame game or focus on what they can't do. As a result, pessimists often become victims of self-fulfilling prophecy.

Why would anyone not want to be an optimist? A Mayo Clinic study indicates that optimists, on average, live longer than pessimists do. The University of Pennsylvania tracked 120 men who had suffered one heart attack. After eight years researchers found that 80 percent of pessimists had died of a second attack compared with 33 percent of optimists. Other research suggests optimism can lead to success at work, in school, and in sports.

In his book *Learned Optimism*, psychologist Martin Seligman studied the New York Mets and St. Louis Cardinals baseball teams. After interviewing managers and players, he predicted the Mets' success and the Cardinals' downfall the following year. Talent being equal, players with a positive, optimistic attitude will outperform those with a negative, pessimistic one.

After the 1995 All-Star Game, I made my annual midseason trip to Seattle to visit with the Mariners team. At the time, Tino Martinez, who had played in the All-Star Game, was struggling at the plate. I found him in the Kingdome, taking batting practice. Tino looked relaxed and happy. Between cuts he joked with Ken Griffey Jr. and other heavy hitters in the Mariners' lineup. Nearby, another player who recently had been called up from Triple A—he had homered in his first at-bat with the big-league club—was having no fun at all. Between pitches he muttered to himself, and after each swing he cursed the result. His body language said he was laboring, pressing. The kid looked as tense as strung wire.

Afterward, I went into the manager's office and shared my observation with Lou Piniella. Tino and the other player provided an interesting study in contrast.

"Mack," Piniella told me, "Tino is like I was when I played. When we struggle we can't wait to get to the yard because we know we're due for a streak. A lot of younger guys who come up start questioning their ability, having doubts. Hitting is all about attitude."

One day I was on a golf course practice green. I spotted Robin Yount, a member of baseball's Hall of Fame. Robin said he couldn't wait for his tee time. He was eager to get onto the course.

"Are you playing well?" I asked, expecting him to say yes.

"No, I've really been struggling," Yount replied. Then he shot me a smile. "But I know I'm due for a breakthrough." When I saw him in the parking lot several hours later, Robin said he had enjoyed a great round.

While a positive attitude doesn't always work, a negative attitude almost always does. Since you don't know what's going to happen, why not act as if you're going to have a good day? If you don't want to believe in positive thinking then just get rid of the negative thoughts.

The Arizona Cardinals had just won a big game on the road. The players were laughing and joking in celebration throughout the long flight home. Much of their playfulness was directed at the flight attendants who moved up and down the narrow aisle taking drink orders and serving dinner. As the plane rocked gently through the night sky, I remember smiling sympathetically at one harried flight attendant whose patience and cheerful disposition had been tested to the limit.

As she walked past where I was seated, she rolled her eyes and muttered a self-reminding mantra of positive affirmation. "I love my job . . . I love my job . . . I love my job . . ."

Attitudes are learned, beginning at a young age. The good news is that attitudes can be unlearned and changed. We can train ourselves to look positively at negative events. I once worked with a UCLA tennis player who hated tiebreakers: *I never win tiebreakers*, she told herself in a negative voice so convincing that she came to believe it, but over time she was able to change her attitude. She replaced that pessimistic voice with a positive one: *I love tiebreakers. Tiebreakers bring out the best in me.*

We learned earlier that you can't outperform your self-image. If you haven't developed a positive frame of mind you're not going to create the mental state that will help you physically perform at your best.

There are three P's for changing pessimism into optimism:

**Permanence.** Optimists believe that when they lose or experience setbacks, these disappointments are temporary rather than permanent.

**Pervasiveness.** Unlike pessimists who let their doubts and troubles affect every area of their lives, optimists are able to put their problems in a "box" and not let them distract them.

**Personalization.** Optimists internalize victories and externalize defeats. *We played great today. We deserved to win. They were lucky tonight. We'll win tomorrow.* The pessimist does just the opposite. *We were lucky to win tonight. It's all my fault we lost. I'm a worthless loser.*

It is said that 10 percent of life is what happens to us and 90 percent is how we choose to react to it. So let me ask you, what kind of attitude do you have? Are you an optimist? How do you view competition, winning, losing, adversity? How do you see yourself responding to pressure?

*Your attitude determines your altitude. If you think you can, or can't, you're probably right. The choice is yours.*

# RIDING THE PINES

*Attitude is a choice. Think positive thoughts daily. Believe in yourself.*
—PAT SUMMITT

*Don't let what you can't do interfere with what you can do.*
—JOHN WOODEN

After starting thirteen games the previous season and being voted by local sports writers as the team's most valuable player, Chris Chandler believed he deserved to be the Arizona Cardinals' starting quarterback. But when the 1993 season began, he found himself on the bench. Coach Joe Bugel had replaced Chandler with Steve Beuerlein, a free agent who had signed a three-year $7.5 million contract.

Bugel's decision wasn't surprising. In fact, it was almost as predictable as cafeteria food. The coach's job was on the line. He *had* to win. Also, in professional sports money talks, and what it says is "Play me."

Hobbled in preseason by an ankle injury, even Chandler wasn't shocked by the move. But the demotion stung him nevertheless. "It's a little embarrassing," he told the media, after the team announced the decision a week before the season opener. "I know I'm not a backup," the new backup said, through gritted teeth.

One day early in the season Chandler approached me as he walked off the field after practice. "How do you handle something like this?" he asked.

As a sports psychology consultant I devote much of my time counseling athletes who are sidelined because of a coach's decision or because they are injured. In this instance, I didn't know immediately how to respond. I wasn't sure what to say.

I liked Chris. The Indianapolis Colts drafted him, then traded him in order to select Jeff George. Then Tampa Bay dumped him in midseason. In my heart I thought Chandler had earned the Cardinals starting job and felt bad for him.

I remembered a magazine article I had read about being your own boss. I told Chandler that even though he was a backup player, removed from the limelight, he still is a commodity on the National Football League stock exchange. ChrisChandlerInc.

Chandler needed to work each day on getting his stock to climb. Having a bad attitude wouldn't help. Not giving his best in practice only would drop his value. I reminded him that he was one play away from being the starter. He had to stay involved and ready. If the club traded him, what would he want the Cardinals coaches and scouts to say about him? He has a good attitude; he works hard; he is coachable; he's a real team player.

Chandler didn't play much that season. The next year he went to Los Angeles and then on to Houston. Eventually he found a home in Atlanta and led the Falcons to the Super Bowl. Good things come to those who stay optimistic and are willing to persevere.

I tell minor league baseball players what I told Chandler. In Triple A, half the players feel they belong in the major leagues. The others think they have nothing to prove at that level. I urged them to "Inc." themselves. They are writing their career résumés with each performance.

It's not easy sitting on the bench—riding the pines. It is doubly tough for athletes who are injured, even though injuries are a part of sports. An athlete can do nothing or use that time of inactivity wisely.

Former Mariners pitcher Erik Hanson says spending more than two months on the disabled list proved to be one of his most valuable experiences in sports. "I didn't just sit around and wait for my arm to get better," Hanson said. "I saw a sports psychologist. At that time, I was just breaking in and was a little inconsistent. I had some good games and bad games, but I really didn't know the batters that well. I didn't know pitching that well and I still don't. Every year is a learning process. I learned ten times more from one night of not throwing a ball than I have my whole life in pitching—all from observing, visualizing, and going through it mentally.

"I'd talk to Nolan Ryan for an hour at a time, to Roger Clemens, and to Mark Langston, who took me under his wing and was very inspirational. These are all guys who have been successful and who train hard . . . and all this was transpiring in the middle of the season during the time I couldn't pitch."

I believe in "can-do" planning. When you're riding the pines, make a list of things you can do. Maybe that means watching videos, studying the opponent, exercising in the weight room, or cheering your teammates on.

Ask yourself what factors you can control and what factors you can't. Many people carry a copy of the serenity prayer. The words are worth remembering.

God, grant me the serenity to accept the things
I cannot change, courage to change the things I
can, and the wisdom to know the difference.

*It doesn't take talent to hustle and work hard. Invest in yourself with a positive attitude and "can-do" thinking.*

# You Gotta Believe

*The biggest thing is to have a mind-set and a belief you can win every tournament going in.*

—Tiger Woods

*When you believe in yourself and the people you surround yourself with, you will win something really big someday.*

—Dick Vermeil

During a practice round Tiger Woods turned to friend Davis Love III and said wishfully, "Wouldn't it be nice if we could play head-to-head down the stretch?" Two weeks later, competing in only his fifth professional tournament, Woods shot 8-under par 64 in the final round of the 1996 Las Vegas Invitational to finish in a tie for first place and force a sudden-death playoff. His opponent was Davis Love.

After the tournament ended on the first extra hole, a television announcer congratulated the twenty-year-old winner on his first PGA Tour victory and asked him if ever in his wildest dreams he imagined being so successful this early in his career.

I'll always remember Tiger's response. The three-time U.S. Amateur champion flashed his thousand-watt grin and replied, without hesitation, "Absolutely."

Golf's newest sensation wasn't being cocky. Tiger was simply sharing the belief he has in himself.

Belief is a state or habit of mind in which trust or confidence is placed in some person or thing. Beliefs drive behavior, and behaviors affect performance in everything we do. When Tiger turned pro and said he expects to win every time—a mind-set he learned from Jack Nicklaus— PGA Tour veterans rolled their eyes. But it wasn't long before Woods opened those eyes to the power of his belief system.

"You realize Tiger means it," Tom Lehman said. "How does that affect me? It changes my mind-set. If I don't expect to win every time, how can I expect to compete? I need to learn what he's learned. I'd better trust in my talent. I'd better believe in myself under the gun. I'd better expect to win."

In psychology, the term self-efficacy is the belief in one's own ability to be successful. Simply believing in yourself doesn't mean you're always going to win. But believing in yourself can help enable you to put yourself into a position to win. Dick Vermeil is one who believed in himself and his players. At sixty-three, he coached the St. Louis Rams to a Super Bowl championship. Another coach, Penn State's Joe Paterno, said, "You've got to believe deep inside yourself that you're destined to do great things."

One year the New York Mets climbed from sixth place to win the National League pennant. "Ya gotta believe!" pitcher Tug McGraw shouted during a clubhouse speech. His words became the motto the '73 Mets carried into the World Series.

The University of Arkansas also enjoyed a successful run during that same era. One year, in celebration of a late-season victory that earned the Razorbacks an invitation to the Orange Bowl, happy Hog fans tossed oranges onto the field. The humor wasn't lost on Lou Holtz. "I'm glad," the Arkansas coach said after the game, "we're not going to the Gator Bowl."

But the Razorbacks' giddiness gave way to gloom. In the Orange Bowl, Arkansas faced Oklahoma, the number-two team in the nation. The Sooners had lost only one game and were coming off a 38–7 rout of Nebraska. Arkansas was a smaller team. Its All-America guard was sidelined with an injury. Also, Holtz benched his top three offensive players for disciplinary reasons.

The media wrote Arkansas's obituary in advance. The Razorbacks, 24-point underdogs, had no chance. Sensing his players were beginning to believe what they read in the newspapers, Holtz called a team meeting two days before the game. He asked his players why they thought they could win. One by one, each stood in the company of teammates and offered a reason. One player cited the Razorbacks' staunch defense. Another reminded that the team's nucleus remained intact. As they spoke, sharing their faith in each other, the atmosphere in the room changed.

Holtz privately told a friend that his team would score 38 points. He was overly optimistic, but not by much. Arkansas won, 31–6.

After the upset victory, a sportswriter remarked how spirited the Razorbacks appeared when they sprinted out of the tunnel and onto the field before kickoff. It looked like a cavalry charge. What had Holtz said to them? "I told them that Oklahoma is big, mean, strong, nasty, and aggressive," Lou deadpanned. "And the last eleven guys out of the locker room are going to be the starters."

Belief systems are a big part of confidence. Beliefs that are irrational or unrealistic lead to stress. Let's look at the **ABC** theory of success and stress.

The **A** stands for the activating event. Tiger Woods enters the U.S. Open at Pebble Beach. **B** is the belief about the event. Tiger tells himself, "I've retooled my game. I've worked hard. I know the course. I'm going to go out and have a good round." **C** stands for consequences, the feelings and behaviors about the outcome. Tiger says, "I felt confident. I played aggressively and smart."

There are several unrealistic or irrational beliefs some athletes have about themselves. Some think they aren't big enough, strong enough, fast enough, or good enough to play at a certain level. My question to them is: "Where's the evidence?" Some have a belief system that says failure is a shameful thing. In truth, life is based upon failures. If you don't fail, you're probably not challenging yourself enough. If, as babies, we had a fear of failure—if we believed that failure is terrible—we might never learn to walk. Another irrational belief is: "If I mess up, no one will love me. I'll be rejected." Imagine the pressure that kind of thinking creates. If you believe that by not winning you're a loser, if you believe that if you lose no one will love you, if you believe that taking a risk is dangerous, if you believe that not being perfect is unacceptable, these beliefs will only cause upset and trouble in your life.

One way some athletes counter irrational beliefs is through positive affirmations. These affirmations should be powerful, positive, and in the present tense. Muhammad Ali was the master. "It's a lack of faith that makes people afraid of meeting challenges, and I believe in myself," Ali said. Also, "To be a great champion you must believe you are the best. If you're not, pretend you are." With a smile in his voice, the former heavyweight champion, and boxing's greatest showman, told himself and the world, "I'm so bad I make *medicine* sick!" Ali proclaimed that there were only two Greats in the world. "Britain and me."

Rod Carew, one of baseball's finest hitters, asked, "Do you believe you're a starter or a bench warmer? Do you believe you're an All-Star or an also-ran? If the answer to these questions is the latter, your play on the field will reflect it. But when you learn to shut off outside influences and believe in yourself, there is no telling how good a player you can be."

In the cartoon strip, Dennis the Menace asks Santa Claus, "Do you believe in yourself?"

Ask yourself that question. What is your belief system? Do you believe in your dreams, your goals, and your abilities? Remember, what your mind can conceive and your heart believe, you can achieve.

*Beliefs drive behaviors and self-limiting beliefs lead to self-defeating behaviors. Believe in yourself and your abilities.*

# BETWEEN THE EARS

*What you are thinking, what shape your mind is in, is what makes the biggest difference of all.*
—WILLIE MAYS

*Competitive golf is played mainly on a five-and-a-half-inch course: the space between your ears.*
—BOBBY JONES

Oftentimes an athlete will go into a performance nosedive. In sports psychology, one means of investigating what happened and why is to retrieve the equivalent of the black box and voice recorder.

I slid the video into the slot and pressed the play button. The major league pitcher seated in my office recognized the figure on the big-screen TV—it was himself. As he stood on the mound and delivered a warm-up pitch, then another, the sights, sounds, feelings, and emotions of that unpleasant day began coming back to him. On the screen, the leadoff batter stepped lightly into the box. Settling in, bat waving back and forth, he turned his eyes toward the figure sixty feet, six inches away.

I then asked the pitcher what he was thinking at that moment, just before the game began.

"I didn't have very good stuff in warm-ups," he began. "I was thinking 'I hope I don't walk this guy.'"

What else?

As he spoke I almost could hear the dread rising in his voice, like water in a flooding basement. "He's really quick. If he gets on, he'll probably take second. Our catcher's arm's not that great. If he steals second there's a good chance they'll score, and we haven't been very good coming from behind . . ."

"Listen to yourself. *Listen*."

The pitcher grinned sheepishly. At the time, he hadn't been aware of his negative thinking. Now he was hearing himself, in his own words, laying out a scenario for defeat. And he hadn't thrown his first pitch! Is it any wonder he performed poorly?

Then, I asked what he *could* have been thinking.

The pitcher studied his image on the screen. "I've got good control of my fastball . . ." One positive thought led to another. "Even if I walk him, I can keep the ball down and get the next guy to hit into a double play . . . Don't worry about the batter . . . One pitch at a time . . . Just focus, relax. Hit the mitt . . ."

We all have conversations going on inside our heads. I call it self-talk. Every athlete hears two competing voices. One is a negative critic, and the other is a positive coach. Which voice we listen to is a matter of choice.

Golfer Arnold Palmer kept this saying in his locker:

If you think you are beaten, you are
If you think that you dare not, you don't
If you'd like to win, but you think you can't,
It's almost certain you won't.

If you think you'll lose, you've lost
For out in the world you'll find
Success begins with a fellow's will.
It's all in the state of mind.

Life's battles don't always go
To the stronger or faster man;
But sooner or later the man who wins
Is the man who thinks he can.

Like our beliefs and attitudes, our thinking can be a powerful ally. How we think affects how we feel, and how we feel affects how we perform. My job is to help athletes think clearly and use their minds effectively by teaching them to turn their negative critic into a positive coach.

One day I was at Yale Field in Connecticut, visiting the Mariners' Double A club, the New Haven Ravens. One of the young centerfielders was struggling in the batting cage. "Mack, I'm never going to get this," he said between cuts. He shook his head. "I don't have a clue." His negative critic was hard at work, shouting into his ear with a bullhorn.

"Let me ask you something," I said. "If Ken Griffey Jr. thought like that, how good a batter do you think he would be?"

The question stopped the kid.

He knew that if Griffey thought the way the minor leaguer did, the Mariners' slugger wouldn't perform well either. The kid's thinking was hurting him more than his swing. He needed to change his thinking, or at least give his mind a rest. Ted Williams offered some sage advice: "If you don't think too good, then don't think too much."

Just as we have irrational and unrealistic beliefs, we all are guilty of distorted and dysfunctional thinking. Atlanta Braves pitcher Tom Glavine said, "I went through the 'Don't do this' syndrome at certain times in my career when facing certain batters. I told myself not to hang a curve ball. Sure enough, I did. Now I focus on 'Do this.' It's a significant difference."

I worked with a professional golfer who listened to his negative critic. Like the pitcher, he watched himself on video. What was he thinking on this shot? How about the next? After listening to his negative narrative, I asked who would be a positive coach for him. He said Ken Venturi. As we returned to the video I asked what Venturi would tell him.

"He would say I'm good enough to do this . . . I can hit this shot . . . Just trust my swing . . ."

Tiger Woods has a positive coach with him at all times. During the last round of the 1999 PGA Championship he faced an eight-foot par putt on the 17th hole. He had to make it to keep the lead. Sergio Garcia was one shot back. As Tiger stood over the ball, he said he heard a familiar voice. It was the soft voice of the man who taught him to play golf. That man wasn't in the gallery. He was several miles away, in a hotel room, watching the tournament on TV. "Trust your stroke," the voice whispered. "Trust your stroke."

Tiger heard and trusted. The putt fell. At the victory party that night, Earl Woods's son said, "I heard you, Pop."

Which voice do you hear? Which is louder, the negative critic or the positive coach? You can choose to listen to the voice that offers and reinforces positive thought. It has been said that thoughts become words. Words become actions. Actions become habits. Habits become character. Character becomes your destiny.

*Mental training teaches you to think clearly and use your mind effectively. Just the way you learn not to swing at bad pitches, you must learn not to chase bad thoughts. Learn to turn your negative critic into a positive coach.*

# Servant or Master

*Learn to control your emotions or they will control you.*
                                                    —Edgar Martinez

*A ballplayer who loses his head and can't keep his cool is
worse than no player at all.*
                                                    —Lou Gehrig

The Philadelphia Phillies had just blown a game against the Houston Astros, surrendering the winning run in the bottom of the ninth. When the manager stormed into the losing team's clubhouse and found his players enjoying a postgame buffet his eyes widened. He felt his blood pressure rise. Suddenly, with a wide sweep of his arm, the skipper cleared the table, sending drumsticks, potato salad, and a tray of assorted fruit flying.

"Boy," a rookie whispered, as the room, splattered with barbecue sauce, fell deathly silent. "The food sure goes fast around here."

Sports arouses emotions and passions like no other endeavor. We see that fervor in highly competitive athletes like Jimmy Connors, who said, "I thrive on emotions. The emotional energy allows me to raise my level of play." We also see it in those who follow sports as spectators. The achievements of one athlete can energize and inspire an entire nation.

Se Ri Pak left her homeland as a virtual unknown. When the young golfer returned to Seoul after winning four LPGA tournaments during her rookie year, thousands greeted her at the airport. The Korean people took her into their hearts. Pak had become a national symbol of triumph over adversity.

Our attitudes, belief systems, and thoughts create our reality. They also create our emotions. Joy is one; pride another. Two other basic emotions are anger and fear. Anyone who has participated in athletics probably has experienced all four.

In "Getting Over Yourself" we mentioned an evolutionary primitive mechanism called the fight-or-flight response. When we feel threatened or stressed, our heart beats faster, our breathing quickens, and our hands may sweat. It's like gulping an adrenaline cocktail. We respond with the urge to flee or fight back. The latter often leads to anger.

Cus D'Amato, who trained Mike Tyson, said emotions, particularly anger, are like fire. They can cook your food and keep you warm, or they can burn your house down. Many great athletes use anger in a positive way. Anger motivates them. Anger steels their resolve. It is much better to become angry than to become afraid.

Last season Randy Johnson was at the plate facing Sterling Hitchcock, who had just given up back-to-back home runs. The San Diego pitcher struck Johnson on the left elbow with a pitch. Johnson flashed with anger. He could have initiated a fight, and risked ejection, but he didn't. Channeling his anger, the Arizona pitcher known as the Big Unit went back to the mound, struck out eleven batters, pitched a complete game, and extended his season record to 7–0.

Albert Belle uses his anger to crush baseballs over the fence. Pete Rose warned, "When you mess with my pride you're going to get into trouble." Michael Jordan is another prideful man. When challenged on the basketball court he exhibited what golfer Sam Snead called a "cool mad." In the playoffs, Jordan was always the smiling assassin.

Sports can be frustrating. It is easy to respond out of anger without thought or control. When he was twelve years old, Bjorn Borg couldn't control his temper. "I was throwing my racquet all over the place . . . hitting balls over the fence—everything," the former tennis great recalled. "My parents were ashamed and finally refused to come to a single match."

Arthur Ashe threw his racquet for the first time when he was ten. Ronald Charity, the man who introduced the boy to tennis, took him to Dr. Robert W. Johnson, a black physician and tennis enthusiast, in Lynchburg, Virginia. The training sessions were long and demanding. In the segregated south during the 1950s, Dr. Johnson knew that tournament directors would kick black kids out of their tournaments if they could find any reason. The Arthur Ashe I played against as a teenager was under control, seemingly imperturbable.

As a youngster, Bobby Jones was beating everyone at the local golf club, but he had a hot temper. He earned the nickname "Club Thrower." Jones became friends with an elderly man everyone knew as Grandpa Bart, who worked part-time in the pro shop. At age fourteen, Jones played in the National Amateur but came home a loser. "Bobby, you're good enough to win that tournament," Grandpa Bart told him. "But you'll never win until you can control that temper of yours."

Jones knew the old man was right, but it was seven years later before he won a tournament. "Bobby was fourteen years old when he mastered the game of golf," Grandpa Bart said. "But he was twenty-one before he mastered himself."

When you let anger get the best of you, it usually brings out the worst in you. Basketball player Latrell Sprewell choked his coach. Roberto Alomar spit at an umpire and became one of the most reviled players in baseball. After Mike Tyson bit Evander Holyfield's ear, he was ordered to undergo a psychological examination.

Uncontrolled anger has led to riots and even death in the sports arena.

A few years ago I was asked to write a sports psychology manual for the Seattle Mariners. I interviewed some of the team's top players. One of them was Edgar Martinez. His manager, Lou Piniella, loves the guy. "Edgar is so professional," Piniella said. "Nothing fazes him. He's as cool as a cucumber at the plate."

During my interview, I asked Martinez what was the biggest jump for him, personally, going from the minor leagues to the majors. His answer surprised me.

"I worked a lot on my emotions," Martinez said. "I don't have a real bad temper, but I can remember some things I've done in the past, like hit the wall or hit the helmet box. But I learned from experienced players that that's not the way you do it. Don't let your teammates or the other team know that you're down or struggling. It's going to hurt your teammates because they're not going to trust you. If you're going to get upset, don't do it on the field. Go into the bathroom, or someplace where you are alone and just let it go. I think that's the best advice I've been given."

Borg soon learned: "A player who cannot control his temper on the court will never become a great player." Jack Nicklaus asks a good question: "How many shots would you have saved if you never lost your temper, never got down on yourself, always developed a strategy before you hit, and always played within your capabilities?"

The best athletes are masters of their emotions and not servants to them. A batter who is controlled by anger and frustration isn't likely to be successful in his next time at the plate. He presses. He feels like he's trying to hit a three-run home run with no one on base.

Pitcher Jim Palmer said whenever he became angry he sat down and tried to analyze what he did wrong and correct it the next time. The legendary Satchel Paige, who pitched in a major league game at the age of fifty-nine, said, "If your stomach disputes you, lie down and pacify it with cooling thoughts."

Simple words. Wise advice.

*Buy the solution, not the emotion. When you let anger get the best of you, it brings out the worst in you. The key question is who is in control—you or your emotions? Remember, before you can control your performance you need to be in control of yourself.*

# FEAR LIVES IN
# THE FUTURE

*Of all the hazards, fear is the worst.*

—SAM SNEAD

*The absolute worst thing a receiver can do is worry about not catching the ball or about getting hit.*

—JERRY RICE

The Phoenix Fire Department is as selective in employment as a professional sports team. Those who want to become firefighters must have the right stuff. Trainees are required to perform many demanding tasks, including climbing the tall ladder, in full gear, used in rescues.

For the past twenty years I have been training booters—firefighting recruits—on the mental aspects of performance. I often give a classroom demonstration. It is a test you can take yourself. If I asked you to stand on the seat of a chair, or on a table top, would you have a problem doing that? Probably not. But what if that chair or table were twenty stories in the air, and I asked you to perform the same task. What thoughts would you have? How would you feel? Could you do it?

The task is the same. So what is the difference? For many, it's a four-letter word. *Fear.*

Fear is a mental response to a perceived danger or threat. As former golfing great Sam Snead said, fear is the worst hazard because it creates tension, doubts, or even panic. While on an African safari, Snead once shot a charging, wild elephant that was thirty yards in front of him. "It didn't hit the ground until it was right at my feet," Snead recalled. "I wasn't a bit scared. But a four-foot putt scares me to death." Fear releases chemical hormones that can inhibit performance and shut you down. When you are afraid in sports you play small. Because you're focusing on the negative, you worry about making mistakes.

I recently played my college roommate in golf. Chris was captain of our college basketball team while I captained the tennis team. We have been competing against each other for almost thirty years, with bragging rights on the line. I'm a much better golfer than Chris. I should beat him. But when he comes to Arizona and we play on my home course, where I should hold a big advantage, I don't perform well. Instead of playing my game, I play it safe. I play not to lose; I play small; I play scared. Fearful of running the ball past the hole and three-putting and losing a stroke to my opponent's handicap, I choke up and leave the first putt short and three-putt anyway. What I've had to learn—what I'm still working at—is not to let fear control me. Stop worrying about making a mistake.

Fear is something we learn as kids. A big coach might yell "You screwed up again!" or "How can you be so stupid?" Youngsters internalize those critical messages. From an early age they would then develop a fear of failure—a fear of doing the wrong thing.

I have great admiration for the Special Olympics program. Its motto is "Let me win. But if I cannot win, let me be brave in the attempt." Coaches and volunteers provide what every athlete needs—encouragement and support. Most Special Olympians, children and adults who are mentally challenged, have no fear of failure when they run a fifty-meter race, do the long jump, or throw a shot put. Fear lives in the future. These athletes live in the present—the here and now. Their participation is fun and rewarding.

Fear reminds me of the Wizard in the magical Land of Oz. It is an unseen presence, a booming voice behind a curtain. Fear is as big and powerful as we imagine it to be. Some athletes resist fear, or some try to deny fear. Others attempt to conquer it. I suggest one shouldn't do any of those things. Fear is a natural part of performance. Former Olympian Bruce Jenner said, "Fear is part of the process. If you weren't scared, you'd be in trouble."

When you resist fear you're only keeping it alive. It's like trying to hold a beach ball under water. The more you fight it, the more pressure you're building up.

Athletes should accept fear and recognize it as the body's way of telling them to become energized. Don't let fear hunt you. Instead, hunt your own fears. Pull the curtain away. Unmask your fears and face them down. Examine them. "Many times when fear starts to hit me, my best chance of overcoming it lies in facing it squarely and examining it rationally," Jack Nicklaus said. "Here is what I say to myself. 'Okay, what are you frightened of? You've obviously played well overall. You're always telling yourself you get your biggest kicks out of the challenges of golf. Well, go ahead and enjoy yourself. Play each shot one at a time and meet the challenge.'"

I once lived alongside the Orange Tree golf course in Scottsdale, Arizona. My house was about 240 yards from the tee box of the 17th hole. It amazed me how often I would find two golf balls in my back yard, one within a foot of the other, both bearing the same company logo. Apparently, one weekend golfer feared slicing his drive out of bounds. His negative thinking helped create the result he feared most. When he teed up the second ball, he worried about making the same mistake and usually did. Al Henderson, a former coach of the U.S. Olympic archery team, said, "Fretting about the shot you just made will get you another just like it."

Jerry Rice, the All-Pro wide receiver, learned how worrying can undermine performance. "I've matured," he said. "When I drop passes, I don't get down on myself the way I did when I was a rookie. On the short drops I used to tense up. I tried to do too much. I started to think too much. Instead of just doing what I had done in practice a thousand times (catch the ball), I worried about dropping the ball."

How does fear limit your life? Your performance? What thoughts accompany your fears? What physical sensations do you experience? Many great athletes who use anger as motivation also turn fear into an ally. Listen again to Bruce Jenner: "I was scared to death, but I made fear score points for me. Fear is right behind me, fear is six inches off my back, that's where fear is. I can feel its presence. But it's not going to catch me . . . I'm going to take fear and use it to my advantage."

Remember, fear doesn't keep you safe. Your training does.

*Don't let fear scare you. Feel the fear and do it anyway. Fear is often false evidence appearing real.*

# BREATHE AND FOCUS

*We all choke. Winners know how to handle choking better than losers.*

—JOHN MCENROE

*You have to learn how to get comfortable with being uncomfortable.*

—LOU PINIELLA

Choker.

It's the ugliest label in sports.

Society views choking in competition as dishonorable, shameful, and unforgivable. Athletes who choke are seen as cowards. Weak-willed. Their moral character is flawed. The Houston Rockets blew a twenty-point lead in the fourth quarter at home against the Phoenix Suns in a 1994 NBA playoff loss. The next day's condemning headlines in both Houston newspapers screamed "CHOKE CITY."

"Why *our* town?" one sportswriter moaned in print. It was as if he took the team's defeat personally. His face burned with shame.

In sports there is no more damning gesture than a mocking hand to the throat, the choke sign. Yet choking suggest athletes who become anxious focus externally. When one of my best friends, Jim Colborn, pitched for the Brewers, he refocused on the task by looking at the flagpole in Milwaukee's County Stadium.

Judge Oliver Wendell Holmes wrote the following about bird hunting, but the advice applies to any athlete in competition: "If you want to hit a bird on the wing, you must have all your will in a focus. You must not be thinking about yourself, and equally, you must not be thinking about your neighbor; you must be living in your eye on that bird."

Choking is nothing more than paying attention to your physiology when you should be focusing on your opponent and the task.

*At times we all get nervous and anxious. Learn to get comfortable with being uncomfortable. Use your breathing to focus your energy. Let your breath center your mind and body in the present.*

happens every day. It happens at Wimbledon. It happens at the Olympic Games. No one is immune.

"We all choke," said golfer Curtis Strange, who won back-to-back U.S. Open championships. "You're not human if you haven't. We get just as nervous as the average guy playing for the club championship." Lee Trevino compares an athlete who caves in to anxiety with a race-car suffering mechanical problems. "Everybody leaks oil."

In 1996 Greg Norman blew a six-shot lead in the final round of the Masters. His fate inspired comparisons with the late-season collapse of the '64 Phillies and the Hindenburg disaster. Last spring Blaine McCallister only had to par the last hole in New Orleans to win his first PGA tournament in seven years. He made bogey. Then he missed a four-foot putt on the first playoff hole that would have clinched the victory. McCallister lost on the next hole to Carlos Franco.

"It had been a long time and the old nerves were going a little bit," McCallister said, when asked to explain his unraveling. "I felt like I bled all over the place out there. I'll be the first to admit I choked it and missed it (on the 73rd hole). It cost me, and I'll hear about it awhile."

McCallister wasn't the only one. A week earlier, Craig Stadler had a chance to win for the first time since 1996. His putter failed him on three playoff holes. He finished second to Robert Allenby at the Houston Open.

Choking is a normal human reaction, a physiological response to a perceived psychological threat. To demonstrate what choking is, I ask athletes to stand and do the breathless exercise. You can do it, too. First, I tell the group this is a contest. I am going to watch each of them and judge everyone's performance carefully. Then I begin barking verbal commands. "Look left . . . look right . . . look left . . . look right . . . look left . . . look right . . . look right . . ." Some automatically dart their eyes to the left, anticipating that command. As they continue the task, their anxiety increases. Their breathing pattern changes. Without realizing it, many hold their breath.

Oxygen is energy—it's juice. Oxygen helps relax muscles and clear the mind. When you hold your breath, you are creating pressure and a nervous feeling. Athletes who choke start to become nervous about being nervous. Anxious about being anxious. One psychologist says anxiety is excitement "without the breath."

The pattern of your breathing affects the pattern of your performance. When you are under stress, deep breathing helps bring your mind and body back into the present.

Over the years I have handed out thousands of little stickers to athletes that read "Breathe and Focus." A baseball player will place the bright orange circle on the shoulder of his uniform or underneath the bill of his cap, or on the barrel of his bat. A hockey player might affix it to his stick. Firefighters I have worked with place the stickers on their self-contained breathing apparatus. The stickers serve as a reminder. Whenever they feel themselves growing anxious, breathe in energy. Breathe out negativity. Breathe in relaxation. Breathe out stress.

One year at spring training, the Mariners tested a new pitcher they had acquired in a trade. The club wanted to see if he could go five innings. In the fifth, he began to fade. He gave up a hit, then another, then another. Seated in the dugout, Lou Piniella turned to me and shook his head. "Mack," Piniella said, "this guy doesn't know how to be comfortable with being uncomfortable." Piniella sent his pitching coach to the mound. When he returned, the coach told Lou, "His eyes are in the back of his head." Translation: the guy isn't there anymore. Piniella took the pitcher out.

What did he mean by learning how to become comfortable with being uncomfortable? Have you ever stepped into a cold shower or icy lake or swimming pool? The cold takes your breath away. Your first impulse is to get out. But if you breathe and stay focused you gradually become accustomed to the water temperature. The experience is akin to performing under pressure. By breathing and focusing you can systematically desensitize yourself.

In addition to changing their breathing patterns, athletes under stress become internally self-conscious instead of externally task-conscious. Their focus turns inward. I

# Be Here, Now

*Each point I play is in the now moment. The last point means nothing, the next point means nothing.*

—Billie Jean King

*You must be present to win.*

—Alex Rodriguez

Alex Rodriguez enjoyed a magical season in 1996. The young shortstop for the Mariners led the American League in batting average, runs, total bases, grand slams, and doubles, and he was runner-up Most Valuable Player, finishing second to Juan Gonzalez of Texas in the closest vote in more than thirty-five years.

Five months later, Alex reported to spring training eager to start anew. Rodriguez is a likable fellow, and his disposition is as sunny as the Arizona sky. I greeted him with a hug. Then I asked about his goals for the coming year. Most athletes are numbers oriented. A ballplayer doesn't have to look up his slugging percentage or earned run average. His stats are like important phone numbers—he knows them by heart. So I expected this twenty-one-year-old to say he wanted to drive in more runs or raise his batting average, which would take some doing. Alex hit .358 the previous year. Instead, his answer floored me and made me smile.

"Bat Mack," Rodriguez said, addressing me by my baseball nickname, "my only goal is to learn how to play one entire game in the present."

To play an entire game in the present moment is the ultimate in mental discipline. Many managers and coaches preach the value of playing the game one pitch at a time or one play at a time. One reason Alex became a star at a young age is because he recognizes the importance of the mental game and understands what it is to play in the present. But the skill isn't quickly or easily learned. The late Bobby Jones, one of the greatest golfers in history, said, "It's nothing new or original to say that golf is played one stroke at a time. But it took me years to realize it."

Successful athletes who speak of "playing in the zone" are describing what it feels like to perform in the present, mind and body attuned, working together. When you are playing your game right on time, in the present, you perform at your best. Why? Because in the present, there is no pressure.

Pressure is created by anxieties about the future and remembered failures from the past. If a baseball player comes to the plate thinking about his last strikeout or says to himself "If I don't start hitting I'll be on the bench soon," is he playing in the present? Obviously, the answer is no.

During an off-season I worked with one of the premier base stealers in the game. What happens, I asked, if while on base he begins thinking about the last time he was thrown out? To make a point, I jumped on his back. I felt like an oversized papoose, but the player got the message. Is it easier to steal a base with a monkey on your back? Thinking about the past—instead of the present—can only slow you down.

In a *Peanuts* comic strip, Lucy is apologizing to Charlie Brown. "Sorry I missed that easy fly ball, manager." In the second frame Lucy says, "I thought I had it, but suddenly I remembered all the others I've missed . . ." In the last panel she diagnoses her problem. "The past got in my eyes!" I would tell Lucy what I tell professional athletes. As you learned earlier, worrying about a mistake will usually get you another one just like it.

One key to learning how to play the game at your best is recognizing when your head is not in the present. I am reminded of the television public service message that asks parents, "It's ten o'clock. Do you know where your kids are?" Ask yourself this: It's game time. Do you know where your mind is?

My definition of awareness is paying attention on purpose without analysis or judgment. Simply put, it is moment-to-moment observation, being absorbed in the task.

Try this. Become aware of your breathing. Count the breaths you take. One . . . two . . . three . . . four . . . five. Repeat the exercise. Do it again. Keep counting. Again. It seems like a simple task, but eventually your mind begins to wander. If your mind isn't on your breathing, what is it on?

I recently had a conversation with a National Hockey League player. He described a game in which he found himself repeatedly glancing at the clock. As the seconds ticked away on his shift, all he could think about was the fact he hadn't scored and time was running out. If he had one eye on the clock, I told him, then he had only one eye on the puck. To be present to win, both eyes have to be on the target—the puck, the ball, the basket, or the job at hand. Let the clock take care of itself.

How do you place your mind in the here and now? When I worked with the Chicago Cubs we used a technique called the mental locker. When a player arrived at the clubhouse at Wrigley Field, or the visiting ballpark, he opened his mental locker. With each article of clothing he removed—his jacket, his shirt, his belt, one sock, then the other—he let go of a problem or a personal concern. By the time he had changed from civilian clothes into his uniform he had shed all his distractions and personal concerns and was focusing on the present. He was in the right time zone and the ideal state of mind to experience success on the field.

Joe Paterno is one of college football's most admired and successful coaches. Every football player at Penn State is familiar with the "blue line" that divides the campus and the school's football complex. Papa Joe tells each student athlete that before he crosses that imaginary blue line on the way to practice or when he leaves his locker for a game, he expects him to dump all his worries and concerns. Once he steps across the line, he cannot be thinking about what grade he made on yesterday's math test or daydreaming about tomorrow night's date. The moment he crosses the threshold, his mind should be focused on Penn State football and nothing else. If it isn't, he is shortchanging himself as an athlete. He is also hurting the team.

He is not fully present to win.

*Learn from the past. Prepare for the future. Perform in the present.*

# Hurry, Slowly

*Be quick but never hurry.*

—John Wooden

*Never hurry when it counts.*

—JoAnne Carner

You can feel the excitement on the first morning of the Griffey International baseball camp. More than two hundred kids, from Alabama to Australia, gather at the Disney World sports complex in Orlando, which is the spring training home of the Atlanta Braves, for five days of baseball instruction and fun. Lined up along the third-base line, the youngsters are wearing their camp T-shirts and big smiles that say they can't wait to get started.

As director of sports psychology for Griffey International, I welcome the kids to the camp and then conduct a contest.

"We're going to find out who the fastest kids in camp are," I tell them. "Now, when I count to three . . . You have to wait for the count. When I count to three I want everybody, all of you, to run to the nearest fence."

Standing at shortstop, I glance at the centerfield fence behind me.

From the smallest to the largest, the campers toe the third-base chalk line in delicious anticipation, motors revving. "Okay, you ready?" I pause for dramatic effect. "One . . . two . . . three! GO!!!"

In a burst of pent-up energy, away they go, dashing straight ahead, legs churning, arms pumping, the wind snatching baseball caps off their heads. After reaching the centerfield fence, the sprinters return, panting and exhausted. Then a comprehending look comes over their faces as they spot about a dozen campers, smiling like the cat that ate the canary and leaning nonchalantly against the fence behind the third-base line. They aren't winded, and they aren't tired. Those few had ignored my non-verbal cue and simply turned around and, as instructed, gone to the nearest fence.

The others feel a little like former NFL defensive great Jim Marshall after he picked up a fumble and ran sixty-two yards into the endzone—the wrong endzone—and scored a safety for the other team.

In sports, what happens when we become anxious and emotionally charged? Most people start rushing. They speed up and get ahead of themselves. A second baseman trying to turn a double play will throw the ball before he has control of it. A wide receiver will turn upfield before he makes the catch.

A pitcher walks a batter and then surrenders a home run at a critical point in the game. Suddenly he and his team are in a hole. His breathing quickens. His heart begins trip-hammering in his chest. Angry with himself, his ego bruised, the pitcher is no longer thinking clearly. His mind starts to race. He takes himself out of his normal rhythm without even knowing it.

When an athlete is in "the zone" everything around him seems to slow down. He feels as if he is performing at an almost leisurely pace. Under stress, the pitcher's world is speeded up like an old silent movie. He feels a rising sense of urgency. He becomes as panicky as the frenetic White Rabbit in *Alice in Wonderland*. "I'm so late! So very, very late!"

In a hurry, his mind no longer in the present, he reverts to what coaches call primitive pitching. Instead of pitching with a purpose, he speeds up. His command changes from "Ready, aim, fire!" to "Ready, fire, aim!"

The pitcher is like a Peruvian tennis player I watched competing in the Davis Cup. The Peruvian was quicker and more talented than his Bahamian opponent. And he was having his way in the match until he got a bad line call. And then another one. He became visibly angry. After that, all his movements appeared hurried. Still simmering, he sailed through the next game so fast I doubt he even knew what he was doing. Unable to regain his composure and slow his tempo he lost the next two sets and the match.

Recall what Jack Nicklaus said in the section entitled "The Pressure Principle." When an athlete tenses up he often wants to get the test over and done with as fast as possible. The more he hurries, the worse he will probably perform. And the worse he performs the more he hurries, creating a self-defeating cycle.

Lee Trevino didn't enjoy playing at the Masters. He said the course didn't fit his game. He complained about the speed of the greens, jokingly suggesting that before each round tournament officials coated them "with STP," a motor oil additive. Trevino plays fast, but he may have set a speed record for touring Augusta National's 18 holes. Frustrated and irritated by his poor play, Trevino barely settled into his stance before whacking his second shot toward the green on the 18th hole. Alluding to the Civil War and the Union general who burned Atlanta, Trevino hurried toward the white, plantation-style clubhouse muttering, "Sherman should have finished the job."

The Arizona Cardinals were in San Francisco to play the 49ers. While seated on the team bus for the ride to Candlestick Park, I noticed a sign above the driver's head. The sign was titled "The First Rule of Holes" and it read, "When you find yourself in a hole, the first rule is to stop digging."

All athletes become frustrated. At some point they all dig themselves into a hole. The best advice I can give is to remember the first rule of holes. If you find yourself in a hole, imagine a red traffic sign that says STOP.

Sometimes the best form of action is inaction. What's the old saying? Don't just do something—*stand* there. What many young athletes need to learn is that sometimes going faster can make them slower. It's one of the paradoxes of sports.

Whenever Seattle pitcher Jamie Moyer finds himself in a hole, when he feels his anxiety rise and he starts to get the gottas—thinking "I gotta do this. I gotta do that"—he knows it's time for him to put the shovel down. Moyer steps off the mound and onto the infield grass. He rubs up the ball, turning it over in his hands. He shakes the tension from his neck. He takes a break and a breath.

The most successful athletes do what Moyer does and what managers do. They call a time out and gather themselves. Earlier we talked about creating a mind gym. Go back to your mind gym and recreate a situation in which you fell into a competitive hole and became overanxious and panicky. Recall how you responded. Then rewrite the script. Visualize taking a time out. See yourself refocusing and returning to the present. Remember, the first step toward regaining composure and tempo is right under your nose—just a deep breath away.

*The more you hurry the later you get. When you find yourself rushing you are no longer in the present. Pace instead of race.*

# Try Easier

*The less tension and effort, the faster and more powerful you will be.*
—Bruce Lee

*The way to run faster is with four-fifths effort. Just take it nice and easy.*
—Bud Winters

Just as Tiger Woods does now, Sam Snead dominated professional golf in his prime because he outdistanced the rest of the field. Snead didn't appear to drive the ball with muscle. On the contrary, the man, who years after retirement age remained so loose-limbed he could bend over and place his palms flat against the ground, was poetry in motion. Snead played golf to waltz time. His tempo was as smooth as the tone in his voice when he addressed his friend on the tee.

"I believe in giving the ball some sweet talk," Snead once said. "'This isn't going to hurt a bit,' I whispered under my breath. 'Sambo is just going to give you a little ride.'"

When Ken Griffey Jr. steps to the plate, he doesn't grind his bat handle into sawdust. "I'm not that strong," Griffey said. "I probably only bench-press about two hundred pounds." The source of his power isn't brute strength, but rather leverage, flexibility, and range of motion. "I don't consider myself a home run hitter. But when I'm seeing the ball and hitting it hard, it will go out of the park."

Sports glorify strength. Coaches demand that athletes give 110 percent, ignoring the fact that it's a mathematical impossibility. Truth is, muscles and strength aren't everything. Over-trying leads to under-performing. Trying harder, which athletes do when they tense up under pressure, oftentimes is counterproductive.

Bud Winters, one of America's most successful track and field coaches, told his athletes, "Just take it nice and easy." Jay Novacek, the tight end on the Dallas Cowboys' early '90s Super Bowl teams, ran track in college. We were working out together one day when Jay told me about an experiment his coach performed. Novacek and his teammates were instructed to run 800 meters as fast as they could. Later, the coach had them run the same distance, only at 90 percent of top speed. "What surprised me, and all of us," Novacek said, "was that our times were better when we ran at 90 percent than when we went all out."

What's the explanation? Voluntary muscles are organized into opposing pairs. Running and many other sports are performed most effectively when some muscles are contracting while others are relaxing. Running at top speed, athletes use all of their muscles—the agonists and antagonists. They are accelerating and braking at the same time. The muscles are at odds. This prevents them from running as fast as they can. Giving 90 percent effort, runners expend a lot of muscular energy but they relax the antagonist muscles that hinder maximum performance.

The same is true in pitching. Trying to throw a ball as hard as he can, a pitcher uses all of the muscles in his arm. But to achieve accuracy and speed, flexor muscles (biceps) need to relax while extensor muscles (triceps) do most of the work.

Nolan Ryan's major league career spanned the administrations of six U.S. presidents. Baseball's strikeout king threw very hard, but he didn't overthrow, which is one reason for his longevity. "The tendency of a fastball pitcher is to muscle up and do what he needs to do," Ryan said. "He winds up lunging and losing his rhythm trying to muscle the ball in there. Everybody has limits. You just have to learn what your own limits are and deal with them accordingly."

My tennis partner, Brad Harper, continually reminds me to relax on my serve. "Mack, spaghetti arm!" Under pressure, we tend to "muscle up." When my arm is loose I'm better able to snap my wrist, and generate more power. Mark Connor, the Toronto Blue Jays pitching coach, demonstrates the physiology by having his pitchers swing a long-handled switch, first with the large muscles in their arm, and then using a quick wrist flick.

Pitchers are taught to grip a baseball as if it were an egg, but in the heat of competition, some squeeze it as if they are choking a chicken. The most common physical cause of error in golf and perhaps all of sports is over-tightness. Over-tightening muscles to produce power actually creates a loss of power and accuracy. Instead of relaxing and releasing, the golfer starts tensing, which hurts coordination. Bobby Jones said that an anxious player's impulse is to steer the ball, which accounts for most bad shots.

In the "Know Your Numbers" section, we compared tension with guitar strings. If the strings are too loose the music is flat; if they are too tight the strings will snap. You should always be able to feel the grip of the bat, the club, or the racquet. If you can't, your grip is too tight. "I wait and wait and let the ball get right on top of me and just swing with a loose grip," says Tony Gwynn, one of baseball's best hitters. If you can't feel your swing, you're swinging too fast or too hard.

Willie McGee once complained to his hitting coach that he couldn't relax.

"Willie," Bernardo Leonard told the player, "an anxious mind cannot exist in a relaxed body. . . . When one is anxious, so is the other. When one is at rest, so is the other."

In the same way you create stress and tension you also can create relaxation. The goal of relaxation training is to teach you how to recognize the early warning signs of tension and to counter or replace them with the sensations of relaxation. Interestingly, one way to relax tense muscles is first to tighten them more. If your shoulders feel like coiled springs, draw them up and squeeze those muscles. Hold the pose for five to ten seconds. Feel the stress and study the sensation. Then release and relax the muscles completely.

If you can relax your body, you can relax your mind. Quiet mind. Quiet body.

*Relaxation happens when you stop creating tension. Over-trying leads to under-performing.*

# SIMPLY OBSERVE

*You can observe a lot just by watching.*

—YOGI BERRA

*It's not between me and the pitcher. It's between me and the ball.*

—MATT WILLIAMS

Years ago while working as a photojournalist in New York, I read a book called *Inner Tennis*. In one chapter author Tim Gallwey shares a simple teaching technique that is rooted in one of the most important principles in sports psychology.

Gallwey describes giving a lesson to a woman who had never played tennis. As expected, she felt nervous and self-conscious. Instead of filling her head with a mental list of commands to remember each time she swung—"Racquet back! Bend your knees! Step in and hit!"—her teacher kept the instruction simple. Gallwey told the student to say "bounce" each time the ball landed in front of her and to say "hit" each time the ball hit her racquet.

Bounce-hit. Bounce-hit. Bounce-hit. When she followed the advice, the student began to relax. She wasn't preoccupied with form and technique, and she wasn't worrying about outcome. Her eyes were fixed on the target. Her mind was focused on the task.

In playing sports we tend to overanalyze. Go to ten golf instructors and you may get ten different verbal cues on how to take the club head away from the ball, initiate hip turn, transfer your weight, keep the left arm straight, and trigger the downswing. Some well-meaning instructors make the game too complex. The old joke is that if golf instructors taught sex education, it would be the end of civilization as we know it.

Part of the brain is always thinking, analyzing, computing, and judging. When I worked with the Cubs, Richie Zisk was the team's bat doctor. His official title was Doctor of Batology. Zisk referred to the overthinking, overanalyzing, critical voice in a batter's head as the "chattering monkey." When you're at the plate or on the tee or on the tennis court and you're listening to all this mental commentary, this verbal static, do you think you can perform at your best? Of course not.

This should be your goal: Play with your eyes, not your ideas.

"I see the ball, I hit the ball," Ken Griffey Jr. says. At the plate he isn't thinking about swing plane or the position of his elbow.

Matt Williams doesn't concern himself with the biography or résumé of the pitcher he is facing. His eyes are zeroed in on one thing—the baseball.

Listen to former pitcher Orel Hershiser: "Once my catcher and I determine the pitch, that's all there is. There's nobody standing there then. I don't think about the next game, the next inning, the next hitter, the next play. There's only the next pitch. It's the only job I have."

Tom Seaver said when he was on the mound he blocked everything out. "Forget that the second baseman just muffed a double play ball. Or that the umpire is missing a lot of calls. Or that your wife just charged $700 at Bloomingdale's."

Bounce-hit. Focus on the target. Set your mind on the task. In the movie *For Love of the Game*, Kevin Costner plays an aging major league pitcher at the end of his career. In his final game, while struggling with fatigue and pain, he uses a mental technique to help him focus on the task. It is triggered by a verbal command. "Clear the mechanism," he tells himself. Suddenly, he becomes detached. He is no longer in Yankee Stadium. He doesn't hear the crowd, he doesn't see the players around him, and he even blocks out the hitter menacingly waving his bat. He isn't analyzing the situation. He is inside a cocoon of concentration. Jack Nicklaus calls concentration "a fine antidote for anxiety." On the mound, the pitcher is in a world of calm. He is living in his eyes, which are trained on the target. All he can see is the pocket of his catcher's mitt.

In his book *Golf My Way*, Nicklaus talks about the single-minded imagery he uses before hitting a shot. "It's like a color movie," Nicklaus writes. "First, I 'see' the ball where I want it to finish, nice and white and sitting up high on the bright-green grass. Then the scene quickly changes and I 'see' the ball going there; its path, trajectory, and shape, even its behavior on landing. Then there is sort of a fadeout, and the next scene shows me making the kind of swing that will turn the previous images into reality. . . ."

It is said the eyes are the mirror to the soul. They also are the mirror to the mind. With great athletes, their eyes aren't searchlights. They aren't even spotlights. They are laser beams.

During a game in Seattle, Arizona Cardinals quarterback Jake Plummer took a beating. The Seahawks' pass rushers sacked him seven times. Late in the game when the young quarterback returned to the huddle, his veteran left tackle, Lomas Brown, gave him a watchful look.

"Jake," Brown said, "lemme see your eyes."

Why the eyes?

"The eyes," Brown said, speaking from experience, "tell it all." Brown could see in Plummer's eyes if the quarterback had lost his confidence or given up. He could tell if Jake was still there, mentally, playing in the present. When an athlete's eyes start to wander so will his mind. Darting eyes are usually not fixed on the task at hand.

Yogi was right when he said you can observe a lot just by watching. In working with athletes, I have them view a videotape of themselves performing at their best. The imagery is more instructive than words. They absorb the images and the positive feelings. They begin to lose their analytical mind and come to their senses.

Do you play with your eyes? How well do you concentrate on the target? Bodybuilder Arnold Schwarzenegger visualizes a specific muscle's contour when he is working out. "A pump when I see the muscle I want," he said, "is worth ten with my mind drifting." One exercise you may find helpful is to pick up an object—a tennis ball, a golf ball, a baseball, or a glove. Hold it; look at it; study it; contemplate it. When your thoughts begin to wander, return your full attention to the object. The exercise will improve your ability to focus and help increase awareness of where your mind goes.

*If your mind starts to wander so will your performance. Keep your eyes centered on the target and your mind set on the task at hand. Focus on the process and let go of the outcome.*

# THE BOTTOM LINE

*The will to win is important, but the will to prepare to win is vital.*

—JOE PATERNO

*Failing to prepare is preparing to fail.*

—WAYNE GRETZKY

Sylvie Bernier had a history of caving in during pressure situations. But now she stood on the top step of the platform, beaming. As the French-Canadian springboard diver turned her eyes to her country's flag and sang the national anthem, the only thing that kept her from rising off the medal stand and floating away like a party balloon was the anchoring weight of the gold medal around her neck.

The experience was everything Sylvie had hoped it would be. From the moment she arrived at the pool, her day went exactly as she had imagined and rehearsed over and over in her mind.

"I knew I was going to dive the sixth of August, at four o'clock in the afternoon in the finals," Bernier recalled in the video *Mind Over Muscle*. "I knew where the scoreboard was going to be—on my left. I knew where the coaches were going to be sitting. Everything was in my head. I knew where the crowd was going to be. I could see my dives exactly how I wanted them to be. When I went to the podium I had seen it before.

"It was like a déjà vu."

The twenty-year-old champion from Quebec won because she came to the biggest event of her life fortified with what every athlete needs.

Confidence.

What do you think is the most important part of the mental game? It's a question I've asked hundreds of managers, coaches, and professional athletes during plane flights and bus rides to stadiums over the past twenty years. The answer is always the same. It's confidence. When you're confident you can relax, trust your stuff, and perform at your best. Confidence is the bottom line.

Where does confidence come from? Great athletes say that confidence is knowing they are prepared physically and mentally. Experience tells them what to do and confidence allows them to do it. Confidence is the *emotional* knowing that you are prepared, mind, body, and spirit, for anything.

Alan Brunacini is the Vince Lombardi of fire chiefs. The head of the Phoenix Fire Department made an interesting comment about confidence. He told me that confidence is knowing what to do when you don't know what to do. Louis Pasteur never fought a four-alarm blaze under a desert sun or coached a team in the Super Bowl, but the words of the nineteenth-century scientist apply to firefighters, football players, Olympic divers, and every other performer. "Chance," Pasteur said, "favors the prepared mind." Or as golfer Tom Kite said, "Give luck a chance to happen."

Throughout this book we stress that mental preparation is as important as physical preparation, if not more so. Television broadcaster Ahmad Rashad, a former All-Pro NFL receiver, said, "Some players with a lot of athletic ability just go out and play. Then after four or five years you don't hear about them anymore. The smart guys figure it out, and they play ten, twelve years. They do it mentally more than they do it physically."

Confidence is the result of preparation, and preparation begins with forming a mental game plan. The great athletes visualize not only best-case scenarios but also worst-case scenarios. They don't imagine failing, but they do mentally plan how they will respond in unpleasant and difficult situations. In sports, the ball takes funny, or not so funny, bounces. Oftentimes games or contests don't go as we had hoped. The prepared athlete has not only a Plan A but also a Plan B and a Plan C.

Reggie Jackson called winning the science of preparation. "And preparation can be defined in three words,"

Jackson said. "Leave nothing undone. No detail is too small."

When our astronauts trained for the first flight to the moon, they rehearsed for everything going wrong as well as for everything going right. If something out of the ordinary happened, they knew how to respond. They over-prepared so they wouldn't under-perform.

During his playing days, former NFL quarterback Fran Tarkenton prepared for the upcoming game by seeing himself, in his mind's eye, performing in difficult situations. "I'm trying to visualize every game situation, every defense they're going to throw at me," Tarkenton said. "I tell myself, 'What will I do on their five-yard line and it's third-and-goal to go, and our short passing game hasn't been going too well and their line looks like a wall and we're six points behind?'"

The marquee athlete uses the mind to program the body. Listen to Nolan Ryan, the Hall of Fame pitcher, describe his routine: "The night before a game I lie down, close my eyes, relax my body, and prepare myself for the game. I go through the entire lineup of the other team, one batter at a time. I visualize exactly how I am going to pitch to each hitter and I see and feel myself throwing exactly the pitches that I want to throw. Before I ever begin to warm up at the ballpark, I've faced all of the opposition's hitters four times and I've gotten my body ready for exactly what it is I want to do."

When you're relaxed, you're in a more receptive state for positive affirmations and visualizations. Steve Carlton, the former strikeout artist with the Phillies, had his own pregame routine. Like Ryan, Carlton would stretch out on a training table and close his eyes. "A lot of people think he's sleeping," said Tim McCarver, who was Carlton's catcher. "But what he's thinking about are lanes in the strike zone. He thinks about the outer lane and the inner lane. He doesn't even think about anything over the middle. And by not thinking about it he gets himself working that way."

ESPN announcer Harold Reynolds used imagery when he played second base for the Mariners. "As I'm running my sprints, I'll listen to the lineup and visualize where I want to play this guy. The night before, I'll make mental and physical notes about how they pitched and played me. I'll write down the guy's move, whether he might want to go right after me or nibble with me. I've got to be ready for that."

Olympic champion Bart Conner mentally rehearsed his performance. In the book *What Makes Winners Win*, Conner said he saw himself as a gymnast doing his routine, feeling the rhythm and the timing. "Then I try to visualize as if I were the person who was standing back and watching me perform," Conner said, "and that's a little different picture. I was always at my best when I saw that picture. It's like once you had visualized it, you see the scene, you see the gym, you see the judges, you see the arena, you see where the equipment is, you see where the chalk tray is, you see everything. So when you actually go to perform, it's like 'Oh, I've been here before.' Then you have such confidence because it's like you've already been through this."

Just as you wouldn't go into a baseball game without taking batting practice, don't go into your competition without taking mental practice. Visualize yourself performing. See the action. Feel yourself moving. Hear the sounds. Smell the smells. Make your images as vivid and clear as you can.

*Confidence comes from the emotional knowing that you are prepared mentally as well as physically. Over-prepare so you don't under-perform.*

# PART IV

# IN THE ZONE

# TRUST YOUR STUFF

*Be decisive. A wrong decision is generally less disastrous than indecision.*
—BERNHARD LANGER

*If there is doubt in your mind . . . how can your muscles know what they are expected to do?*
—HARVEY PENICK

On the day of the final round of the 2000 Masters tournament, Vijay Singh received a nice surprise, the kind of surprise that touches a father's heart, the kind that brings a smile. Singh's nine-year-old son, Qass, had pinned a note to his dad's golf bag. The message read, "Poppa, trust your swing."

Not wanting to disappoint the boy who trusted in his father, the leader did as requested. Playing steadily and confidently, from the first hole to the last, the man from Fiji whose first name means "victory" won the Masters by three shots. Afterward he appeared with Qass at the champion's press conference wearing the green jacket and a triumphant smile.

"That's what I tried to do," Singh said, reflecting on his round. He looked at his son. "Trust my swing."

Successful athletes trust their talents. They are committed to every swing, every stroke, every shot, and every pitch. When asked for golfing tips, I tell friends that the best advice I can give is that it's better to be decisive than right. The late Harvey Penick, one of the game's most revered instructors, said if you are indecisive, if you have doubts, if there is a lack of commitment in your mind, how is your body going to know what to do? We all have seen what can happen to the most talented athletes. Under pressure, they sometimes become tentative and indecisive. They don't trust their stuff.

One such scene played out during a sudden-death playoff at the Masters in 1990. It was almost a gimme. Only two feet stood between Scott Hoch's ball and victory. He lined up the winning putt from one direction. He walked behind the hole and gave it a second look. Hoch came back, knelt behind his ball, and studied the line awhile longer. Then he took another look.

It was twenty-four inches—tops—almost straight in, but Hoch looked like pool shark Minnesota Fats circling a green felted billiard table, chalking his cue, and reading every angle before making a four-bank trick shot.

It was growing late. Instead of unconsciously speeding up, as some athletes do under stress, Hoch slowed down. Chi Chi Rodriguez said, "Take less time to read the scorecard and more time to read the hole." Good advice, but Hoch read the hole as if it were *War and Peace*. Finally, the golfer stepped up to his ball. Settled into his stance. Eyes flicked anxiously from ball to hole, hole to ball, back and forth.

Watching on TV, Ben Crenshaw, conscious of the passing time Hoch had spent—fifty-five seconds and counting—was on the edge of a scream.

"Geez," Ben said, "*hit* it!"

At last, Hoch drew back the putter blade. There was more prayer than conviction in his stroke. Click. The ball slid three feet past the hole. Crenshaw flinched and shook his head. "Like my dad says," Ben said in disbelief, "Good God-o-mighty!" Hoch went on to lose to Nick Faldo, who birdied the second playoff hole.

Doubts cause intellectual confusion. Doubts can be paralyzing. It is said that a person who doubts himself is like a man who would enlist in the ranks of his enemies and bear arms against himself.

Confidence and trust are essential in every sport. Hall of Fame pitcher Sandy Koufax of the Dodgers said it is better to throw a poor pitch wholeheartedly than to throw the so-called right pitch with a feeling of doubt. "You've got to feel sure you're doing the right thing. Sure that you want to throw the pitch that you're going to throw."

Today's Dodgers' ace, Kevin Brown, says that if you make a bad pitch aggressively you have a much better chance of getting away with it.

The habits of success are forged in practice. In practice you learn the art of concentration. "You can be out there in the middle of a tough match pleading to yourself, 'Concentrate! Concentrate!' and it won't happen for you," said Martina Navratilova, the former tennis star. "Concentration is born on the practice court . . . you must mentally treat your practice sessions as matches, concentrating on every ball you hit."

In practice you learn to train your brain as well as your body. Sam Snead said practice time is when you put your brain into your muscles. The conscious practice of routines leads to the unconscious habits of success. A routine is something you do regularly that you control and has a purpose. Before Nomar Garciaparra steps into the batter's box he begins a series of fidgety gestures, repeatedly tugging on his batting gloves. Taking his stance, he taps one toe and then the other against the dirt. They are the same quirky habits he performs in practice. Every hitter has his own routine. Routines are comforting mechanisms—triggering mechanisms. They differ, however, from rituals based upon superstition, like Wade Boggs's habit of eating chicken at 3 p.m. before every night game.

In golf, a preshot routine begins with the player standing behind the ball, looking at the target. In a thinking mode, it's time to analyze and develop strategy. Ask yourself questions. Where is the pin? What direction is the wind blowing? It's the time to mentally shape the shot, as Jack Nicklaus described.

Once you have decided how you are going to play the shot, and you step up to the ball, it's time to get your head out of the way so your body can perform. Turn off the analytical mind. Switch from the thinking mode to the trusting mode. You can't be thinking and swinging at the same time.

Ask yourself this: Are you better than your stuff? No. So just trust it.

*You must be 100 percent committed to each action. If there are doubts in your mind, your muscles won't know what to do. Let your routines switch you from the thinking mode to the trusting mode.*

# WHITE MOMENTS

*Each time I step on the basketball court, I never know what will happen. I live for the moment. I play for the moment.*
—MICHAEL JORDAN

*When I'm in my groove there is no thinking. Everything just happens.*
—OZZIE SMITH

en Crenshaw was as surprised as anyone when he broke par in the opening round of the Masters in 1995. A day earlier, he had been in Austin, Texas, attending the funeral of Harvey Penick, his ninety-year-old teacher and lifelong friend. Harvey gave Crenshaw his first golf club when Ben was six. Over the years Harvey always was there, offering his pupil encouragement and simple teachings that expressed a philosophy that went deeper than mechanical advice. After burying his dear friend, Crenshaw flew to Augusta National. When he arrived he felt tired, hollow, washed out. He was emotionally spent.

"I don't know what to expect," Crenshaw said before teeing off. Four days later, what he never imagined would happen, did.

At age forty-three, eleven years after his last win at the Masters, Ben won again. When the final putt fell, Crenshaw bent over and hid his face in his hands and wept.

"I still reflect on it so much," Crenshaw said five years later. "So many unexplained things happened that week. I hadn't played worth a darn in a good while but I gained a lot of confidence that first day and it kept going. I was very relaxed, but determined, too. In many respects I felt like I was a kid again . . . I played by instinct the whole week. I was as calm as I've ever been."

Many people who play sports long enough or work at their craft hard enough experience those magical moments where their training and trust in themselves come together in perfect harmony. Their performance flows smoothly, effortlessly, and almost unconsciously. This heightened level of performance—Michael Jordan described it as the reward for years of hard work and preparation—is unexplainable. Sometimes these special moments seem to happen as if by grace.

Perhaps you have experienced a competition when everything falls into place, like tumblers in a wall safe. You feel like pinching yourself to verify you're not dreaming. At times you want to break out laughing, while telling yourself, "This is unreal. I'm not *this* good!" But at that moment and place, you are.

All great athletes know the feeling. They use different words to describe it. They're on autopilot; they're tuned in; in total control; in the groove; locked. Japanese baseball players have their own word for it. *Mushin.* Loosely translated, it means "no mind." Tennis star Arthur Ashe called it "playing in the zone."

"The zone is the essence of the athletic experience," said former NFL player Dave Meggysey, "and those moments of going beyond yourself are the underlying allure of sports."

The moments are rare and illuminating. Yuri Vlasov, the former world champion Russian weightlifter, wrote verse when he wasn't training. His illustrative description of the "zone" experience reflects the soul of a poet. "At the peak of tremendous and victorious effort," Vlasov said, "while the blood is pounding in your head, all suddenly becomes quiet within you. Everything seems clearer and whiter than before, as if great spotlights had been turned on. At that moment you have the conviction that you contain all the power in the world, that you are capable of everything, that you have wings. There is no more precious moment in life than this, the white moment, and you will work very hard for years just to taste it again."

Athletes in every sport occasionally experience being in the zone. Former NBA player Byron Scott said, "All you can hear is this little voice inside you, telling you 'shoot' every time you touch the ball. Because you know it's going in."

As a Phoenix Sun, Charles Barkley scored 56 points in a playoff game against the Golden State Warriors. In the first quarter, he made eleven field goals in a row, layups, jump shots, three-pointers, from all over the court. No misses. As one shot fell, then another, then another, his teammates along the bench were on their feet, grinning and shaking their heads. Joe Kleine made a circle with his arms, as if to indicate the rim was the size of a hula hoop. After Barkley drilled in a flat-trajectory jumper over a defender, the Suns star turned to the Warriors' cheerleaders huddled under one basket. His grin said, "You ain't stopping me. Not tonight."

The late Jim "Catfish" Hunter accomplished the ultimate as a pitcher with the Oakland A's. "I wasn't worried about a perfect game going into the ninth," he recalled. "It was like a dream. I was going on like I was in a daze. I never thought about it the whole time. If I'd thought about it, I wouldn't have thrown a perfect game—I know I wouldn't."

When you're in the zone, you have switched from a training mode to a trusting mode. You're not fighting yourself. You're not afraid of anything. You're living in the moment, in a special place and time. As a certified hypnotist, I see similarities between people who are in a trance and those in a performance zone. At age thirteen, Tiger Woods worked with a sports psychologist who taught him how to use hypnosis to block out his conscious mind and to strengthen his resolve and focus. Skills in hypnosis helped the young golfer go to such deep levels of concentration that he couldn't remember making certain shots. Tiger told *The New York Times Magazine*, "You ever go up to a tee and say, 'Don't hit it left, don't hit it right?' That's your conscious mind. My body knows how to play golf. I've trained it to do that. It's just a matter of keeping my conscious mind out of it."

Athletes who are playing in the zone experience time distortion. Everything seems to slow down. Describing a peak performance, NBA star Reggie Miller said, "It all seemed to happen in slow motion." In tai chi they call it falling through a hole. The awareness of the passage of time completely stops.

Others experience size and space distortion. "The ball looked like a grapefruit," or the basketball rim was a hula hoop.

Athletes in the zone see everything with clarity. They are relaxed, they perform with a quiet mind, with no indecision and no doubts. They can almost anticipate what is going to happen. They are totally absorbed. Golfer Tony Jacklin likened the zone to being in a cocoon. Dave Winfield said, "I'm in my world." Payne Stewart said, "When it happens, all you see is the ball and the hole."

Have you experienced "white moments"? Can you recall a time when you weren't concerned about the opponent or the outcome and were simply living in the moment and performing at your best?

There is no better feeling in sports.

*The harder you try to get into the zone the further away you get. The zone is the reward for all your hard work and preparation. Just go with the flow and enjoy the moment.*

# PARALYSIS BY ANALYSIS

*Slumps are like a soft bed, easy to get into and hard to get out of.*

—JOHNNY BENCH

*A full mind is an empty bat.*

—BRANCH RICKEY

Several years ago the Cubs selected Rick Wilkins in the first round of the draft. The young catcher was labeled a can't-miss prospect. To use a sports cliché, his future was all ahead of him, which is where the future should be. While playing for Peoria in the Class A Midwest League, Wilkins began struggling at the plate. Forget hitting a baseball. "I couldn't hit the broad side of a barn with an oar," the youngster said, voicing his growing frustration after a loss.

The next day I went to Peoria, Illinois, at the Cubs' request, to work with the farm club. That afternoon I gave an inspired talk to the Chiefs team about the mental aspects of performance. The players and coaches really got into it.

That night Wilkins looked like a different player. The kid belted a first-inning home run. In the third inning he doubled. Later, he added a sacrifice fly. "What a difference a day makes," Wilkins said, beaming after the game. "I just saw the ball well and let the bat go." Next morning, the headline in the local newspaper read something like "Cubs Shrink Helps Phenom Out of Slump."

I felt gratified and proud until I spoke with Wilkins the next day. He told me he had missed my talk because of a dental appointment.

Sports is a roller-coaster. It's a series of performance peaks and valleys, ups and downs, twists and turns. If an athlete's best day is a "zone" experience then the worst day is one in which he or she is muddled in a slump—a natural cycle in sports. While we associate the word slump with baseball, athletes in all sports experience times when they feel as if they can't do anything right.

The University of Tennessee football team once beat Alabama 24–0. It was the first time an Alabama team coached by Bear Bryant had failed to score in 115 games. The Crimson Tide attempted fifty-one passes, but the Volunteers picked off eight of them. In the huddle, an Alabama wide receiver who hadn't lost his sense of humor suggested to his quarterback that he try throwing one to a Tennessee linebacker, "and I'll see if I can intercept it."

Golfer Ian Baker-Finch won the 1991 British Open and then went into an extended slump. His game just left him without a note of good-bye. At times, other athletes have felt as helpless and perplexed as the major league rookie who stopped hitting and went to a veteran teammate for advice. The old pro suggested that the youngster switch to a twenty-nine-ounce bat.

"Will it help?" the kid asked hopefully.

"No," the veteran said. "But it'll be lighter carrying back to the dugout." The old joke is that there are many theories on conquering slumps. Unfortunately not one of them works.

Some athletes deal with slumps by denying their existence. After he broke a 0-for-20 drought, Dave Henderson claimed, "I wasn't in a slump. I just wasn't getting any hits." Yogi Berra didn't blame himself when he wasn't hitting. He blamed his bat. If his woes continued, he changed lumber. "I know it sounds silly," Berra said, "but it keeps me from getting down in the dumps. . . . It keeps my confidence up."

Billy Williams, a hitting instructor with the Cubs, likened a slump to a traveling illness. "A slump starts in your head and winds up in your stomach. You know that eventually it will happen, and you begin to worry about it. Then you know you're in one. And it makes you sick."

Sometimes slumps can be traced to physical problems or mechanical glitches. But oftentimes the problem is all in the mind. Athletes who begin to struggle start over-analyzing. They hear that monkey Richie Zisk talked about, chattering in their head. They start thinking too much. In a *Peanuts* cartoon, Snoopy commends Woodstock on making a perfect landing on the roof of his doghouse. Then he begins quizzing the tiny yellow bird about aerodynamics. "Now when you take off again, do you push with your feet? Or do you flap your wings first? Do you flap your wings and sort of lean into it, or do you . . ." In the next panel, Woodstock has disappeared, having dropped straight to the ground with a "Klunk!" after takeoff. Snoopy put the lesson learned into words: "If you *think* about it, you can't do it."

A former ballplayer didn't mean to sound funny when he said of a slump he was in, "I've been doing my best not to think about it, but by trying so hard not to think about it, I can't stop thinking about it."

Overthinking often leads to over-trying. "When you're in a slump you start going up to the plate trying to hit a home run," major league outfielder Cory Snyder said. "You start pressing instead of just letting things happen. You let all the negatives come floating through your mind."

Not long ago an NBA player came to me during a low point in his career. Nagging injuries had affected his long-range shooting. His field-goal percentage dropped dramatically. Media scrutiny added to the pressure and frustration he felt. His answer for combating his slump had been to work longer and harder in practice. I urged him to relax, rest his body, and get his mind off the game for a couple of days. Get away from basketball. Take his wife and children on a picnic. In an attempt to regain his form, he was digging himself deeper into a hole and needed to put the shovel down.

Years ago, when I was a director at St. Luke's Medical Center in Phoenix, I met Karl Kuehl, who was then head of player development with the Oakland A's. Kuehl had spent a lifetime in the game, as a player, scout, coach, and manager. He shared with me his views about the mental game of baseball, which became the title for a book he coauthored.

Kuehl once asked a major leaguer what he would be concentrating on in the game that night. The player was hitting an anemic .226 at the time.

"I want to get a couple of hits and drive in a couple of runs," the player said.

Kuehl reminded him that a hitter doesn't have control over whether he gets hits or drives in runs. Karl is right. Instead of being outcome oriented, a hitter should concentrate on what he can control. Focus on having quality at-bats. What is a quality at-bat? It means relaxing, seeing the ball well, and being patient. The difference between a .250 hitter and a .300 hitter in the major leagues is only one hit a week.

The key to overcoming a slump is finding a difference that will make a difference. Usually this means doing less rather than more.

*Sports is filled with ups and downs. Remember the first rule of holes is to stop digging. Go back to basics and keep things simple.*

# PARADOXES OF
# PERFORMANCES

*To succeed in baseball, as in life, you must make adjustments.*
— KEN GRIFFEY SR.

*Sometimes you have to get worse before you get better.*
— TOM WATSON

W hy are boxing rings square? Why is the foul pole fair?

These questions illustrate the contradictory and paradoxical nature of sports.

A paradox is defined as a seemingly contradictory statement that may nonetheless be true. After Steve McKinney broke the world downhill ski record he said, "I discovered the middle path of stillness within speed, calmness within fear, and I held it longer and quieter than ever before." Whenever I think about paradoxes I recall Muhammad Ali's heavyweight title fight against George Foreman in Zaire, Africa. Who would have thought that a boxer could win by inviting his opponent to hit him, the more times the better? But that's what Ali did. For

seven rounds Ali leaned against the ropes and allowed—encouraged—his powerful young opponent to flail away with a barrage of body punches. The "rope-a-dope" strategy worked. In the eighth round, with Foreman arm-weary and exhausted, Ali abandoned his defensive posture and sent George spinning to the canvas with a left-right combination.

Ali's strategy seems as contradictory as the idea of going over a high jump bar upside down. Dick Fosbury turned his back to the bar before jumping over it at the Olympics in Mexico City. The American won the gold medal and his innovative new technique, which became known as the Fosbury Flop, has been used by almost every high jumper since.

Sports is always changing. The forward pass changed football forever. The jump shot changed basketball. Metal woods, an oxymoron, have changed golf, and oversized racquets have changed tennis.

Just as games change, athletes must be willing to make changes and adjustments. This isn't always easy. Try this: Fold you arms in front of you. Now unfold them and fold them again, this time the other way. It feels awkward, doesn't it? It doesn't feel natural. As we talked about earlier, by making needed adjustments in your game your performance may suffer temporarily. You have to be willing to get worse before you can get better, which is one of the paradoxes of sports we will discuss.

Sports is a game of balances. An example I use is that people who are sick take medicine to get well, but too much medicine can be poisonous, even fatal. In school, kids are taught that if they don't succeed, then try, try again. I tell athletes, yes, try again. Don't give up. But maybe try something different. Perhaps do the opposite—a 180-degree turn. Many coaches are rigid and inflexible in their thinking. Everything is black or white. It isn't. Sports can be both black and white, like the Oriental yin-yang symbol. I try to teach any performer to play in the gray, and to understand and accept the paradoxical nature of sports.

Let's examine ten paradoxes.

**Less can be more.** Sometimes the highest form of action is inaction. Athletes require rest and recovery time. Without it, they become stale, burned out, and more susceptible to injuries. In this book we quote Vince Lombardi saying, "The harder you work, the harder it is to surrender." So how can not working as hard as possible be an advantage?

One year the Arizona Cardinals had lost three games in a row. The coaching staff's response was to practice more. You see that with many coaches. They believe that if the team isn't winning, the players aren't working hard enough. So the NFL team worked out on Thanksgiving Day. The players didn't want to be there. Their minds

were on family and turkey dinner. The team went through a half-hearted practice and its star defensive back, Tim McDonald, blew out his knee and missed the remainder of the season.

**The harder you try to get into the zone the further away you get.** We talked about this in the "White Moments" section. Train hard, but then let the performance flow naturally. Don't try to *make* something happen, just trust your stuff and *let* it happen.

**Trying easier can be harder.** Many athletes put too much muscle into their performance in an attempt to create power. Oftentimes over-muscling is self-defeating. Remember the golfer's prayer: "God, grant me the strength to swing easier."

**Over-control gets you out of control.** Or you can gain control by giving up control. When pitchers become too cautious and controlling with their pitches they often start aiming and steering the ball with unhappy results. Performance improves when they surrender to the process. You often see this on the golf course, too. A weekend player having a miserable round gives up hope. That's when he suddenly sinks the forty-foot putt or hits his longest and straightest drive of the day. Why? He is no longer trying to control his swing.

**Slowing down can make you faster.** Jay Novacek learned this paradoxical truth while training with his college track team. Pace instead of race. Be quick but never hurry. I once worked with a golfer trying to qualify for the U.S. Open. Instead of arriving in plenty of time before his morning round, he showed up later than planned. He started rushing, and as a result he didn't play his best. Shortcuts often take you the wrong way.

**Fear of failure makes failure more likely.** Fear creates tension and affects coordination and rhythm. The chances of success are diminished. Oftentimes a team that puts together a winning streak becomes preoccupied with not losing. Once the streak ends, and the house of cards falls, players breathe a sigh of relief. "Now," they tell themselves, and each other, "we can start over and concentrate on winning one game at a time."

**Playing it safe can be dangerous.** Or the greatest risk sometimes is not to take a risk. Figure skater Michelle Kwan played it safe in her final performance at the 1998 Winter Olympics. Tara Lipinski, the underdog, held nothing back and skated a more difficult routine, and then won the gold medal. Kwan later won the world championship by going out and letting her performance flow. By playing it safe, athletes are reluctant to make the adjustments necessary to move up to the next level of competition. A pitcher with a funky curve ball will strike out the side in Class A. But that same pitch will be lunch meat in the big leagues. Improvement requires letting go of old ways.

**A step backward is a step forward.** Sometimes you have to get worse to become better. Tiger Woods stepped back when he retooled his swing. He and his coach, Butch Harmon, believed that in the long run Tiger would become a more consistent and better player—which he has.

**The probability of getting the outcome you want increases when you let go of the need to get it.** The more you want to achieve a goal, the more expectations you place upon yourself. Greg Norman wants to win the Masters more than any other tournament. He may want to win too badly, which, some theorize, is the biggest reason why he hasn't, despite coming very close. Give yourself permission to win, but then let go of the idea of winning and focus on execution and the process.

**While you must be present to win, you also have to be absent to win.** Athletes who experience those "white moments" lose their conscious mind. They are wrapped in a cocoon. They are living in the moment.

*Understand the paradoxical nature of sports. Learn to play in the gray. Sometimes you have to get worse before you get better.*

# CHOICE NOT CHANCE

*Consistency is what counts. You have to do things over and over again.*
—HANK AARON

*The greatest and toughest art in golf is "playing badly well." All the greats have been masters at it.*
—JACK NICKLAUS

Invariably, the question will come after I've lipped out three putts in a row, or as I'm walking off the green—shaking my head with my blood pressure pushing the red line—after making double bogey. A member of our group will turn to me and casually ask, "So, Gary, what do you do for a living?"

In those self-conscious moments I hate admitting that I'm a professional sports psychology consultant. I know what he must be thinking. *THIS guy gets paid to help people with their game?* If I'm playing poorly and the question comes, I'll paste on a smile and say, "When you counsel yourself, you have a fool for a client."

What fascinates—and frustrates—me as a golfer is the unpredictability of performance. One day I can shoot 75, which is a good round for me. The next day, playing on the same course and using the same clubs, I may shoot 85.

Which player will I be today? Jekyll or Hyde? When he plays badly, Bob, a golfing buddy, laughingly tells me, "My evil twin showed up today."

Sports psychology is especially prescribed for two kinds of athletes. Some perform well in practice but break down in competition because they become self-conscious or overanxious. Others possess worlds of talent but can't perform consistently. Consistency separates good athletes from great ones. The best athletes win consistently because they think, act, and practice consistently.

Consistency is a defining quality. "Whatever your job, consistency is the hallmark," said Joe Torre, manager of the world champion New York Yankees. "It's much more important than doing something spectacular just once. Do your job consistently, and you will be considered good."

What made Chris Evert a champion? "My father's coaching, training, and persistent encouragement paved the way," said the former tennis great. "But it was something more: I was consistent over a long period of time because I never looked back, never dwelled on my defeats. I always looked ahead."

The greatest athletes are those who can perform at a high level day in and day out, even when they don't feel well or they are off their game. As Jack Nicklaus said, it is an art to "play badly well."

Closing pitcher Dennis Eckersley didn't always have his good stuff. On those days, he performed a little mental trick. "You fake it," Eckersley said. "You do. You can't let on that you're not throwing well. There's a body language. I really believe it. You've still got to act like you're the man. You can't fake a good fastball. I'm not saying that. But you have to give the impression that your stuff is on time."

It's like the television antiperspirant commercial—never let them see you sweat. Albert Belle says he can sense if a pitcher is confident or feeling a little shaky by the way he carries himself. We reveal much of our thoughts and emotions through body language. In a *Peanuts* cartoon, Charlie Brown is standing with his head bowed, looking at his shoes. "This is my depressed stance," he tells Lucy. In the next panel, he draws his shoulders back, chin up. "The worst thing you can do is straighten up and hold your head high because then you'll start to feel better." In the last panel Charlie Brown assumes his woe-is-me pose and says, "If you're going to get any joy out of being depressed, you've got to stand like this."

Joe DiMaggio said, "You ought to run the hardest when you feel the worst. Never let the other guy know you're down."

Chris Evert boiled inside when she played. If her confidence was shaky, or she was losing her composure, she worked very hard not to show it. "If you give in to your emotions after one loss you're liable to have three or four in a row."

Every athlete has bad days. The trick, Arnold Palmer said, "is to stay serene inside even when things are going badly outside." Sam Snead believes that to achieve consistency, a golfer must put a distance between himself and what happens on the course. It's not indifference, it's detachment. Jim Colbert echoes Snead's advice. "My reaction to anything that happens on the golf course is no reaction," Colbert says. "There are no birdies or bogeys, no eagles or double bogeys. There are only numbers. If you can learn that, you can play this game."

Ben Crenshaw says that in golf you take the lies as they come. "Take the bad bounces with the good." Have you ever hit a terrible drive and then followed it with a miraculous recovery shot out of the trees, landing the ball on the green? Don't act surprised when you do something well, and when you're struggling don't let others know it.

Maintain the warrior mentality. Stand tall even if you feel you are coming apart on the inside, and carry yourself in a confident way. All performers can act themselves into a way of thinking just as they can think themselves into a way of acting. Mental attitude is always important. As a player, Dave Winfield, a member of the 3,000-hits club, knew that what he thought affected how he felt and how he felt affected how he performed. "Sometimes you have to say to yourself that you're going to have fun and feel good before you go out there," Winfield said. "Normally, you have fun after you do well, but I wanted to have fun before I did well. And that helped."

*To perform consistently you must prepare consistently. Act the way you want to become until you become the way you act.*

# INNER EXCELLENCE

*The quality of a person's life is in direct proportion to their commitment to excellence, regardless of their chosen field.*
—VINCE LOMBARDI

*My baseball career was a long, long initiation into a single secret: At the heart of all things is love.*
—SADAHARU OH

Early in his career Shaquille O'Neal and his United States teammates traveled to Athens, Greece, to compete in the World University Games. A writer asked the seven-foot-one center if, during his visit, he had checked out the Parthenon.

"No," O'Neal replied. "I haven't been to all the clubs yet."

Since that time the world has seen basketball's man-child mature as an athlete and a person. Shaq's biggest growth spurt came at age twenty-eight during his eighth pro season, when he led the league in scoring, finished second in rebounding, placed third in blocked shots, and led the Los Angeles Lakers to a league best 67–15 record and the National Basketball Association championship.

During the season O'Neal thought of a boat trip in Montana he took with his uncle the previous summer. Shaq knew his new coach, Phil Jackson, had a vacation residence near the river, and during the trip he found it. In a window overlooking a dock, O'Neal spotted the championship trophies that Jackson's Chicago Bulls teams had won. "Six gold balls," O'Neal recalled. Gleaming in the sunlight. "They blinded me." In truth, their sparkle opened his eyes.

On the day he received his own shiny trophy, the 1999–2000 NBA Most Valuable Player Award, the most dominating player in the game said he wanted to be nicknamed "Big Aristotle" because, in his words, "It was Aristotle who said, 'Excellence is not a singular act but a habit. You are what you repeatedly do.'"

Obviously not everyone who reads this book is going to become a world-class athlete like those quoted in these pages. But each of us can be an MVP—a Most Valuable Person.

It doesn't take exceptional talent, education, or wealth to become an MVP. One becomes an MVP by achieving excellence within. Inner excellence is a way of thinking and a way of acting. It is a quality of mind, a mentality that says no matter how difficult things become, you are responsible and accountable for your thoughts, feelings, and actions. Inner excellence is staying positive in negative situations, and it is dealing with adversity in an optimistic way. It is finding love and joy in what you do and remaining steadfastly committed to your goals, values, and dreams. It's staying cool when the heat is on.

People with inner excellence look at competition as a challenge. They are motivated by a desire to succeed rather than by a fear of failure. They possess an unconditional, high self-esteem and self-image. They have a can-do attitude and a will to prepare to win. They believe the harder they work, the harder it is to surrender. They don't quit or play the blame game, and they look after the smallest detail to go the extra mile. They are big enough to back down from trouble and strong enough to be kind, fair, and honest.

Excellence goes beyond winning and losing. Inner excellence can't be taken away by a referee or an opponent or the final tick of a scoreboard clock. Western society is externally oriented; we're always going outside of ourselves to find validation and heroes and to measure success. We look outside for what only can be found inside. An MVP works on the inside, knowing that it will show on the outside.

Let's review ten qualities of inner excellence.

**The person who is a winner within has a dream.** Eleanor Roosevelt said the future belongs to those who believe in the beauty of their dreams. Remember Dwight Smith's sensory-rich dream of playing for the Chicago

Cubs? Imagination is like life's previews of coming attractions. Pursue your dream. Turn that dream into action through goal setting.

**Commitment.** MVPs are committed to their goals. They live their lives on purpose. They are Ted Williams as a boy, wishing upon a star and dedicating himself to reaching that sky's-the-limit goal of someday being known and honored as the best hitter ever to play the game. "I hated every minute of training," Muhammad Ali said. "But I told myself, 'Don't quit. Suffer now and live the rest of your life as a champion.'" Joe Frazier, Ali's opponent in three epic bouts said, "You can map out a fight plan or a life plan, but when the action starts, it may not go the way you planned, and you're down to your reflexes—your training. That's where your roadwork shows. If you cheated on that in the dark of morning, you're getting found out now, under the bright lights."

**Responsibility.** Those who achieve inner excellence are response-*able*. They don't let what they can't do interfere with what they can do. Like Notah Begay, they take responsibility for themselves and their actions. There is a footnote to the story about losing my job with the NFL Cardinals. After Buddy Ryan was fired after only two seasons, the organization invited me back. If I hadn't swallowed my anger and disappointment—if I had burned my bridges—that probably wouldn't have happened.

**Openness to learning and growing.** An MVP turns weaknesses into strength. Remember from *Mr. Baseball* the Japanese word *kaizen*, which means constant daily improvement? Learn how to play with the paradoxes of sports. We don't grow old. We get old by not growing.

**Optimism.** A positive mental attitude is essential to becoming the hero that is within you. Chris Chandler could have quit football, but he never lost faith in himself. An optimistic spirit helped Andre Agassi climb from the bottom of the world rankings to number one in 1999. "I've always learned so much more from my downs than my ups," Agassi said. "They're really who I am."

**Self-confidence.** No one can outperform his or her self-image. Athletes with inner excellence, like Tiger Woods, believe in themselves and their abilities. They know how to do within when they're doing without. Part of responsibility psychology is knowing that no one can take away your self-esteem without your permission. Have the courage to growup and fulfill your potential.

**Emotional control.** In coaching life skills to professional athletes I am careful not to come off sounding judgmental. Rather than make accusations, I pose questions: "Do you think that was appropriate? Does thinking like that serve you well? Do you think that was a real mature thing to do?"

**The adversity quotient.** An MVP looks at obstacles as opportunities and views setbacks as springboards for comebacks. MVPs see stumbling blocks as stepping stones. "Keep your head up," Paul "Bear" Bryant advised his college players. "Act like a champion."

**Those with inner excellence possess the backbone of character.** They practice good sportsmanship. "Success without honor," Joe Paterno said, "is an unseasoned dish; it will satisfy your hunger, but it won't taste good." Former coach Gene Stallings said you can't go wrong by doing right. While that may sound trite, it's true. Pick people up; don't put them down; walk your talk; live by your principles. If you don't stand for something, you can fall for anything. If you stay in the middle of the road, the chances of getting hit are doubled.

**An MVP is persistent and patient.** Don't give up on your dream. Don't let others dissuade you. Hang out with people who stoke your fire, not soak your fire. When times are good be grateful, and when times are bad be graceful.

*Working on the inside shows on the outside. What lies ahead of us or behind us is of little matter to what lies within us.*

# THE HERO WITHIN

*Every time your back is against the wall, there is only one person that can help you. And that's you. It comes from the inside.*

—PAT RILEY

*It's not the size of a man, but the size of his heart that matters.*

—EVANDER HOLYFIELD

During the 1998 WNBA finals against Houston, I walked into the Phoenix Mercury locker room before the game. Written on the chalkboard of the club that would fall one shot short of winning the title was a quotation from Ralph Waldo Emerson: "A hero is no braver than the ordinary person. He is just braver five minutes longer."

Sports is more than a contest of physical ability. As the ancient Greeks knew, sports also test courage, which comes from the Latin word meaning heart. And it's the human heart where the hero within us lives.

The rich tapestry of sports is woven with the threads of heroes. Playing from the heart, people overcome adversity, beat the odds, or take their game to a new level. Some stories read like fairy tales. Cinderella stories, we call them. In 1995 Kurt Warner was bagging groceries in Iowa for $5.50 an hour. Five years later he earned the National Football League's Most Valuable Player Award and led his team to victory in the Super Bowl. His bags-to-riches story is as inspiring as the song I play for athletes at the end of every training session. The song, by Mariah Carey, is titled *Hero*.

Bernard Malamud, author of *The Natural*, said without heroes the rest of us don't know how far we can go in life. "If I can be a source of hope to anybody," Warner said after being named the Super Bowl MVP, "I'm proud to be a part of it."

Competitive sports can bring out the best in people. Instead of playing small, they overcome their self-doubts and fears. They let their light shine. They find courage, which is the opposite of discourage, and tap into their reservoir of potential. Reflect a moment. Can you remember a time when you were a hero, when you showed heart, courage, and fearlessness that maybe you didn't think you had?

I like what Dr. Thad Bell had to say. An assistant dean at the University of South Carolina medical school, Bell was at one time the world's fastest human over the age of forty. "You can rise above almost any obstacle if you're willing to work hard and believe that you can do it," he said. "I want everyone to remember that ordinary people can do extraordinary things."

There is no mold from which heroes are formed. They come in all sizes, all shapes, all ages, and all walks of life. During a discouraging time in my career, I saw a television interview with an Olympic hopeful who had lost a leg in a car accident. After grieving, she said she decided to become the best one-legged skier in the world. I didn't feel so sorry for myself anymore.

Jean Driscoll is a six-time Boston Marathon winner in the wheelchair division. In the book *A Hero in Every Heart*, Jean describes "jogging" with President Clinton, at his invitation. "He told me that I have the best-looking arms in America," Driscoll said. "In fact, when he gave me his autograph, he wrote, 'To Jean, the best-looking arms in America.' Some people think that successful persons are born that way. I'm here to tell you that a champion is someone who has fallen off the horse a dozen times and gotten back on the horse a dozen times. Successful people never give up."

Most heroes don't make the nightly television newscast, or appear on the sports page. The world doesn't hear about the spirit of folks like Elwood Ware. The seventy-year-old farmer fell out of a pecan tree. When his son found him four hours later, Ware was unconscious. He had broken his leg and five ribs. The farmer spent six months on crutches. But neither Mr. Ware's age nor the hitch in his get-along mattered when he picked up a discus at the Texas Senior Games and threw it as far as he could. "It didn't matter if I won," the septuagenarian said, showing off his silver medal. "Thing is, I tried it."

Sis Warnke, a retired school teacher, took up running after turning sixty-two. At age seventy-eight the grandmother from Las Cruces, New Mexico, showed up at the Arizona Senior Olympics wearing a pair of sneakers and a cap that spoke of her spirit and good humor: "GET EVEN," the words said, "Live Long Enough To Be A Problem To Your Kids." Sis ran the 440, the 880, and the 1,500 meter races.

Before Paul Westphal became an NBA coach, he took a job at Southwestern College, a small Bible school in Phoenix. The school didn't have a gym. When Westphal interviewed for the position he asked the president if the school had any players. The president smiled and told Westphal he had passed them in the lobby. "I thought that was the tennis team," Westphal recalled. "They were all five-foot-ten white guys." One of them was a substitute named Tim Fultz.

Fultz made the team for two reasons. First, Westphal didn't cut a player if he worked hard, and no one practiced harder than Tim. Also, the team needed transportation and Fultz had a car—a beat-up bomb.

Southwestern's season came down to a rematch against Arizona College of the Bible. A victory would send the

Eagles into the national tournament. Late in the game two of Westphal's starters fouled out. With forty seconds left, the coach had no choice but to send in Fultz.

As expected, the other team immediately fouled the inexperienced substitute, putting him at the line. Fultz missed both free throws. Fouled again, he missed two more. With ten seconds left and Southwestern's lead cut to three points, guess who got fouled again?

Fultz stepped to the line, heart pounding. First shot, good. Second one, swish. That night the team carried the unlikely hero off the court on its shoulders as players and fans chanted his name. A minister's son, the young man later became a missionary in Zaire. While roofing a new church, he fell thirty-five feet and later died. Tim Fultz's heart was transplanted and now beats in the chest of an African man.

*The world of sports reveals many heroes. So does everyday life. It takes courage to grow up and reach your full potential.*

# THE WELL-PLAYED GAME

*Sports can do so much. It's given me confidence, self-esteem, discipline, and motivation.*

—MIA HAMM

*Successful competitors want to win. Head-cases want to win at all costs.*

—NANCY LOPEZ

The late Tom Landry, former coach of the Dallas Cowboys, said sports are a great teacher. I wholeheartedly agree. The world of sports is both a classroom and a laboratory. Through competition we learn from a young age the value of training, practice, and discipline, as well as the meaning of fair play. Sports teach us how to persevere. How to deal with adversity. How to become part of a single heartbeat that defines a team. Sports teach lessons in leadership, respect, and courage.

In sports, unlike other, more vague areas of life, there is a scoreboard, time limits, rules, and a level playing field. When Jackie Robinson broke the color line in major league baseball, former executive Branch Rickey reminded the future star that a baseball box score is democratic. It doesn't tell how big you are, what church you attend, what color you are, or how your father voted in the last election. "It just tells what kind of baseball player you were on that particular day."

Runner George A. Sheehan compared sports to the theater ". . . where sinner can turn saint and a common man can become an uncommon hero. . . . Sport is singularly able to give us peak experiences where we feel completely one with the world and transcend all conflicts as we finally become our own potential."

At the recreational level, sports are about doing your best and having fun. Unfortunately, coaches, parents, and even young athletes (who take their cues from adults) often forget the purpose of competition. They look at professional sports, which is a business—winning and losing translates into dollars and cents—and lose perspective. Youth coaches scream at kids and kick the dirt in anger, imitating big-league managers. They behave as if coaching Little League is their livelihood. They lose sight of what's most important at this level— success is measured not in wins and losses but in the personal growth and development of young players.

Roger Staubach, the former Cowboys quarterback, said, "The only successful youth sports program is the one with the coach who will accept the losing along with the winning, last place in the league along with the first place, and still be able to congratulate his team for their efforts."

But how many coaches do that? The behavior of some coaches and moms and dads leaves you wondering who is more mature, the adults or their ten-year-olds.

In Alvin, Texas, Nolan Ryan's hometown, a police sergeant who is an assistant coach on a Pony League team for thirteen- and fourteen-year-olds was ejected for arguing a close call at first base. He went home, put on his police uniform, returned to the ballpark, and waited for the game to end. When the umpire left in his car, the officer stopped him and gave him a warning ticket, saying the umpire had failed to signal. For this stunt, the officer was demoted and put on six-month probation. The umpire later said, "This was all real juvenile, over a baseball game."

The policeman/coach should have been with me last summer at the Goodwill Baseball Series in Japan. In Asia respect for the game is very important. Players at the high school level bow to the umpire. They also bow to the field. It is a sacred time and place. Today we hear kids say "Don't be disrespecting me." If the game of baseball and other sports could talk they might be saying the same thing. Sadly, we have gotten away from civility and good sportsmanship.

A survey of five hundred adults in five Florida counties showed that 82 percent believe parents are too aggressive in youth sports. A North Carolina soccer mom was charged with hitting a teenage referee after a game, and a Cleveland father punched a fifteen-year-old boy on the soccer field because he said his son was being pushed around by the bigger player. In Massachusetts the fathers of two ten-year-old hockey players came to blows during a game. One man died from head injuries. In Jupiter, Florida, an athletic association required grown-ups to take a class in how to be good sports. Parents were instructed to watch a nineteen-minute video on the roles and responsibilities of a parent of a youth athlete. They also signed a code of ethics pledging to behave at sporting events.

Americans are obsessed with winning. In our society, if you don't win then you're a loser. Fans are unforgiving. In Philadelphia, the City of Brotherly Love, sports fans are said to be so tough that when the local teams aren't in town they go to the airport and boo bad landings.

When your favorite team wins, you feel energized. Even the food tastes better. TV announcer John Madden had a good line: "Winning is a great deodorant." When I was in graduate school at Arizona State University, social psychology students counted the people wearing caps, sweatshirts, and jerseys bearing the ASU logo after football games. They found that the number of fans wearing the school colors was 30–40 percent higher after the Sun Devils won than after they lost. It is called the BIRG syndrome—Basking In Reflected Glory.

We need to redefine winning. Vince Lombardi said winning isn't everything but making the effort to win is. A winner is one who walks away from competition knowing he has done his personal best regardless of placement, rank, or standing.

"Being the first to cross the finish line makes you a winner in only one phase of life," said Ralph Boston, a former track and field Olympic gold medal winner. "It's what you do *after* you cross the line that really counts."

We also need to examine the mixed messages from professional sports. The National Hockey League claims it doesn't condone violence but the assaults on some players on the ice would qualify as a crime if they occurred on the street. The National Football League fined former Arizona Cardinal safety Chuck Cecil $30,000 for two acts of "flagrant unnecessary roughness" involving the use of his helmet against the Washington Redskins. Yet each season NFL Films splices together a collection of greatest hits and puts them to music. Violence is glamorized.

What does the well-played game mean to you?

Do you believe it's not cheating if you don't get caught? Is inflicting injury a justifiable part of the game? Your philosophy about sports determines how you play the game.

*Play hard. Play clean. Play fair. Play your best.*

# GAME DAY

*I'm a totally different person on the mound than I am on the street.*

—NOLAN RYAN

*I won't even call a friend the day of a match. I'm scared of disrupting my concentration.*

—CHRIS EVERT

Five hours before game time on a bright, late-spring afternoon, a solitary figure sat alone in the stands behind first base in Anaheim Stadium. Walking toward him, crossing the manicured grass in right field, I thought how strangely quiet and wonderfully peaceful it seemed, so different from the last time I was in the stadium, when the Arizona Cardinals played the then Los Angeles Rams. That memorable Sunday afternoon the raw roar of the crowd filled the arena. Standing on the sideline, I could hear the grunts, the violent slap of pads, and the voice of Cardinals special teamer Ron Wolfley, black paint smeared under each eye, as he came off the field, half-crazed: "Forget the refs!" Wolfley screamed. "It's jungle rules out there!"

Now, several months later, I crossed the ball field and climbed the stadium steps. The man wearing his uniform pants and a T-shirt motioned for me to sit down and join him.

Jim Lefebvre, manager of the Seattle Mariners, sat in silence, taking it all in—the warming sunshine, the perfect geometry of the diamond, the peacefulness. "Mack, listen how quiet it is," Lefebvre said. "It's like a church. A temple."

Sitting there I thought of Annie Savoy's soliloquy from the movie *Bull Durham*. "I believe in the Church of Baseball," Annie said. "I've tried all the major religions and most of the minor ones—I've worshipped Buddha, Allah, Brahma, Vishnu, Siva, trees, mushrooms, and Isadora Duncan. I know things . . . For instance, there are 108 beads in a Catholic rosary. And there are 108 stitches in a baseball . . . I've tried them all and the only church that truly feeds the soul, day in and day out, is the Church of Baseball."

Lefebvre gazed at the field. The sweep of empty stands. "This place has got a rhythm to it. It's like a heart beating. *Buh-bump.*" As the manager imitated the sound of a single heartbeat, he closed and opened his right hand. "In forty-five minutes our guys will come out for batting practice. Then the vendors will start showing up. *Buh-bump. Buh-bump.* And the fans will start to arrive, and the other team will come in, and you can see them over there

208

in the dugout. *Buh-bump-buh-bump-buh-BUMP.*" Jimmy's hand opened and closed, opened and closed, faster now. "Then the lights go on and the umpires step onto the field and they play the national anthem." And in his mind's eye, Lefebvre could see it, and feel it, as surely as he could feel his own pulse, the baseball game, a living, breathing thing.

Sports is not life and death, but it has been called war without fatalities. On game day the heart quickens, and competitive athletes put on their "game faces." I have seen it in all sports. With some athletes it's almost a Jekyll–Hyde transformation. Mild-mannered soccer star Mia Hamm described her game-day mind-set as a "warrior mentality."

Hank Aaron said the most important thing is how a person prepares to do battle. Everyone gets ready differently. Bo Jackson, the greatest specimen of an athlete I've ever seen, is a soft-spoken fellow. I worked out with him in Phoenix when he was rehabilitating his hip, which he injured playing in the NFL. Jackson described his alter ego as Jason, the indestructible evil force in the *Friday the 13th* movies. "I refuse to let him out of his box," Jackson said. "Except on Sundays in the fall. I let him out on Sundays when I strap my helmet on and go out and play football."

Alex Karras, the former Detroit Lions star, assumed a bigger-than-life identity on game day. He became Paul

Bunyan, the giant lumberjack. "I wake up in the hotel room in the morning," Karras said, "and I say to myself, 'Paul, we're going to have ourselves a game this afternoon. We are going to remove the stuffings from people.' I can feel myself inflate."

Larry Wilson, former general manager of the Arizona Cardinals, is a quiet, soft-spoken man. Looking at him, one never would guess that he was one of the hardest hitters in the history of professional football. A member of the Pro Football Hall of Fame, Larry invented the safety blitz. I asked him one day about the fierceness with which he played on Sundays. "On game day I thought about being on a ranch again, punching cattle," Wilson told me. "If anybody came into the pasture where my cattle were, they were rustling. They were going to get punished. And they wouldn't want to come back again."

In the NFL, players review films on Monday, Tuesday is a day off, on Wednesday the coaches put in the game plan, and by Friday players mentally begin funneling down. They start eliminating the world around them and focusing on Sunday's approaching kickoff. Some check into a hotel two days before the game. They get so keyed up they don't want to be around their wife and kids.

On game day many professional athletes put on dark glasses and headphones and listen to music to help insulate them from the outside world. Music helps energize or calm them down. The music is as varied as the personalities on a team: jazz, gospel, rock, or rap. Long before viewers turn on their TVs to watch an NFL game, the warriors are mentally and emotionally girding themselves for battle. Many go into the stadium early and stroll up and down the field, a practice known as "grazing."

Some find strength and comfort in worship. When the Phoenix Suns played the Chicago Bulls in the NBA Finals, Charles Barkley walked into the Suns clubhouse and found it empty. He knew his teammates were holding a pregame prayer service in another room. Barkley picked up a felt-tipped marker and wrote his game-day theology on the message board: "God helps those who help themselves."

Great athletes strive for balance in their lives. On game day they find the warrior within. They know when and how to turn it on, and when the game is over they know how to turn it off.

*When the lights go on, it's showtime. Be prepared mind, body, and spirit to do battle with everything you have, so when the contest is over you can leave the game behind with no regrets.*

# THE MIRROR TEST

*When the game is over I just want to look at myself in the
mirror, win or lose, and know I gave it everything I had.*

—JOE MONTANA

*The softest pillow is a clear conscience.*

—JOHN WOODEN

At age nineteen the pride of Commerce, Oklahoma,
arrived in the big city wearing a Sears Roebuck suit
and carrying a cardboard suitcase. He was *The Natural* in
the flesh. He could do it all and he did. He beat out drag
bunts. He snagged Gil Hodges's deep drive to left centerfield to save Don Larsen's perfect game in the 1956 World
Series. He hit a ball 565 feet. He became the greatest
switch-hitter in the history of baseball. He was number
seven of the Yankees—an American icon and my boyhood hero.

Growing up in New York, I called him Mickey, as if I
knew him personally. I imitated his swing from both sides
of the plate. Kids coveted and collected his baseball cards.
I still have a ball he autographed during his heyday, when

fans of all ages worshipped him, before injuries and surgeries broke him down.

By any measurement, Mickey Mantle was hugely successful as an athlete. But Mantle was an alcoholic. In the spring of his second season with the Yankees, after his father died of Hodgkin's disease, he started drinking. For forty-two years Mantle blotted himself out with the bottle and abused his body. He failed as a husband and a father. At banquets and in bars, Mantle recited a line that always got a laugh. "If I'd known I was gonna live this long, I'd taken better care of myself."

But the joke wasn't funny. Alcohol ruined his liver. Sadly, Mantle's biggest wins came very late in life. He won his biggest World Series when he checked into the Betty Ford Center and became sober. His most important home run was reconnecting with his family. As Mantle told *Sports Illustrated*, fifteen months before he died of cancer, "I'm going to spend more time with all of them—show them and tell them I love them."

Serving not only as a performance coach but also as a personal counselor, I see athletes backstage, unguarded, away from the applause, and out of the white glare of the limelight. Some professional athletes who appear to the public to have the world on a string actually lead unhappy lives. Sports heroes are human, too. My boyhood idol had feet of clay. But while Mantle's story is a sad one, I have experienced the joy and satisfaction of watching other sports figures develop and grow as athletes and as people. One of my favorite success stories is Ken Griffey Jr.

I've known Ken and his father since 1987. Junior was seventeen when the Seattle Mariners chose him from Cincinnati's Moeller High School in the first round of the draft. Two years later he made it to the big show. One of the game's greatest players, Griffey passes a test I ask all athletes—and will ask you as a reader—to take. It's the Mirror Test. "I'm a big believer in the mirror test," said John McKay, the former NFL and college coach. "By that I mean that you shouldn't worry about the fans or the press or trying to satisfy the expectations of anyone else. All that matters is if you can look in the mirror and honestly tell the person you see there that you've done your best."

Ken Griffey Jr. enjoys the peace of mind that comes with looking at his reflection. "As long as I can look in the mirror and know I've done everything I could," he said, "that's all I care about."

A poem I like says, in part:

When you get what you want in your struggle for
   self
And the world makes you king for a day
Just go to the mirror and look at yourself
And see what that man has to say.

You may fool the whole world down the pathway
   of years
And get pats on the back as you pass
But your final reward will be heartache and tears
If you've cheated the man in the glass.

Harvard researchers collaborated on a project to define what makes a successful life. They produced a list called the Five L's.

**Love.** For a performer, love is the most basic ingredient for success. Without love for your sport and those people who are important to you, you aren't living. You're only breathing. As Peggy Fleming, the former Olympic champion figure skater, said, the most important thing is to love your sport. Never compete just to please someone else. "You've got to love what you're doing," hockey great Gordie Howe said. "If you love it, you can overcome any handicap or the soreness or all the aches and pains." Listen to former major leaguer Ozzie Smith: "Now that I'm out of the game I know how lucky and blessed I was to play the game that I loved." When he coached for the Chicago Cubs, former star Jimmy Piersall said the first thing he did before the start of every spring training was to fall in love with the players and the game all over again.

**Labor.** It is said that if you do what you love, you never work a day in your life. But there is no shortcut to success. Success is built upon dedication and hard work. Red Auerbach, the legendary Boston Celtics coach, valued work ethic as much as he did talent. He quizzed players about their work habits. How did they respond to coaching? How could they improve upon their talent? "Take Larry Bird," Auerbach said. "He doesn't have the speed. He doesn't have the height. But he works and works, shoots and shoots . . . He sets inner goals for everything—for the week, for the month, for the season."

**Learn.** Frank Howard, the ex-big-league slugger, said the trouble with baseball is that by the time you learn how to play the game, you can't play it anymore. The same could be said for most other sports. Dan Fouts, the NFL Hall of Fame quarterback, compares an athlete's career with the scales of justice. "The left side of the scales is piled full of talent and the right side is piled with brains. When you begin your career, it's full of the physical and almost void of the mental," Fouts said. "Then as you get further along . . . the balance shifts to the mental side as your physical abilities deteriorate and your mental capabilities accelerate. The frustrating thing is, you can see your body aging right before your eyes, but you know so much more about the game and how to play it. That's really the way I always felt, especially as I got past the middle of my career. I felt I can't play forever but I'm learning more every day." I tell young athletes that they should learn from the mistakes of others because they won't have time in life to make them all themselves. Manager Lou Piniella tells players that they have to remember their mistakes and then forget them.

**Laughter.** Don't let competition kill your sense of fun. Part of the music of sports is laughter. Someone asked former manager Whitey Herzog what it takes to be a success in his business. "A sense of humor," Whitey replied, "and a good bullpen." After an embarrassing loss, John McKay was asked about his team's execution. "I'm all for it," the coach deadpanned. During the 1998 season, Mariners pitching coach Bryan Price was working with prospect Ivan Montane, a hard-throwing but inconsistent right-hander. The Cuban pitcher was wearing a necklace made of bones. When Price ordered Montane to take off the good-luck charm, the pitcher warned that if he did, it would cause Price's death. "I'm not scared of dying," Price replied. "I'm scared about getting fired if you pitch bad again." Life is too important to take too seriously. If you learn to laugh at yourself you will enjoy a lifetime of entertainment.

**Leave, or let go.** "I know that I'm never as good or bad as any single performance," Charles Barkley said.

"I've never believed my critics or my worshippers, and I've always been able to leave the game at the arena." Former manager Sparky Anderson warned that winning can become an unhealthy obsession. "The trick is to realize that after giving your best, there's nothing more to give. . . . Win or lose the game is finished. It's over. It's time to forget and prepare for the next one." Love the game, or your work, but don't be married to it.

I see the five L's in Ken Griffey Jr.'s life. He loves baseball. He works hard. He's a learner and a student of the game. He has fun. And although he wore a Seattle Mariners uniform for eleven years, he was able to let go and move to Cincinnati and continue his career in the city where he grew up.

Success in life is peace of mind, the feeling of having no regrets. It comes from knowing you did your best. Everyone eventually leaves the game. Imagine for a moment you're attending a testimonial dinner in honor of your retirement from competition. Maybe you're retiring after high school or college or at the end of a professional career. Maybe you're a weekend warrior. Your friends are at the banquet and so are all your coaches, former teammates, and those you competed against. Each one stands up and says a few words about your character and how you played the game.

What would they say?
What would you *want* them to say?

*Success comes from the peace of mind of knowing you did your very best on and off the field as a player and as a person. When you leave the game how do you want to be remembered? How do you define success?*

# THE BIG WIN

*I'm proof that great things can happen to ordinary people if they work hard and never give up.*
— OREL HERSHISER

*I may win and I may lose, but I will never be defeated.*
—EMMITT SMITH

Hobbled by foot injuries, Mark McGwire missed most of the 1993 and '94 seasons. Each of those years he hit only nine home runs. When the slugger, who then played for Oakland, suffered another setback the next spring, he wondered if the baseball gods were trying to tell him something. Frustrated and worried about his future, he turned to family and friends for advice. They urged him to give it at least one more year.

Imagine if McGwire had quit baseball. Think of what he and all of us would have missed. McGwire would never have hit home run number sixty-one on his father's sixty-first birthday and written his name alongside Roger Maris in the record book. He never would have shared this memory with the St. Louis Cardinals batboy— McGwire's ten-year-old son. As Big Mac circled the bases, Matt McGwire stood at the plate, waiting to be swept up in his dad's embrace. What a moment—three generations joined by one home run.

If McGwire had quit, he never would have hit number sixty-two—a feat that thrilled him so much that he forgot the first rule of Little League: touch them all. In his excitement, McGwire missed first base. He came back, touched first, touched second, touched third, and touched home. The night McGwire took ownership of the most prestigious record in sports, he touched everything and everyone.

If McGwire had quit, baseball's new Man of Steel wouldn't have hit five home runs during the last forty-four hours of the magical 1998 season. Before his last at-bat, he stood in the on-deck circle, eyes closed, absorbing the energy. Then he stepped to the plate and belted number seventy. They say that seventieth baseball is worth thousands. But how can you put a price tag on that heroic summer and the impact it made upon the game, the fans, and the country? McGwire said it all: "I can't believe it, can you?"

Michael Jordan's goal as a teenager was to make his high school basketball team. He can still see himself back then, as an anxious sophomore, on the long-awaited day when his coach posted the typewritten sheet in the gym. The students who made the team were listed, while those left off had been cut.

Jordan's eyes searched the list. He ran a finger down the alphabetical column of names. His wasn't there. His heart sank. After school that day, Jordan went home, shut himself in his room, and cried hard tears.

Thankfully, determination overcame disappointment. The skinny youth refused to accept he wasn't good enough. He didn't give up. If he had, we wouldn't have experienced the pleasure of watching the greatest performer in basketball history win NBA championships and MVP titles and lead a "Dream Team" to gold on the Olympic stage.

Lance Armstrong remembers the moment doctors gave him the grim news. In 1996 the cyclist was told he had testicular cancer. The disease had spread to his abdomen, brain, and lungs.

"The first thing I thought was 'Oh, no. My career is in jeopardy,'" Armstrong told friends. "Then they kept finding new problems. I forgot about my career. I was more worried about making it to my next birthday."

Armstrong underwent four rounds of chemotherapy and had surgery to remove brain tumors. Remarkably, less than three years after doctors gave him only a 40 percent chance to live, the twenty-seven-year-old Texan was pedaling fiercely across France, over the Alps, and across the Pyrenees. Bent over his two-wheeler, the American led the way on the 2,286-mile journey over some of Europe's most extreme terrain. Up hill and down dale, in sunshine and in rain.

Some climbs were as steep as the steps of a football stadium. He ate on the go. He sipped liquids, like a hummingbird from a feeder. Fueled by willpower, he was a sewing machine, burning six thousand calories a day.

The Tour de France is one of the world's greatest tests of human endurance. The race has been compared with running a marathon every day for twenty days. Lance Armstrong doesn't need a trophy to prove he is a winner, but he received one in 1999 anyway. On the last day of the race, he arrived in Paris, draped in an American flag, and embraced by cheers, the winner. But more than that, Armstrong is an inspiring symbol of survival. His is a life-affirming story and continues to be. Lance repeated the feat the following year.

In working with athletes, and all performers, I remind them that we don't know what the future holds for any of us. So why not act as if you're going to have a great future? Set your goals. Do the work. While positive thinking doesn't always work, negative thinking, unfortunately, almost always does.

Throughout this book we have talked about some of the world's best-known athletes. Most champions, however, aren't famous. They aren't written about in *Sports Illustrated* or interviewed on ESPN; instead, they are all around us. They are everywhere we look.

Ida Dotson was two years old before her parents suspected something was wrong. Tests confirmed that the child from Tombstone, Arizona, was hearing impaired.

When Ida turned four, her mother and father drove to Tucson and placed her in the Arizona School for the Deaf and Blind. She spent ten years at the school.

Her sophomore year, Ida said she wanted to go to public school, so she enrolled at Tombstone High. She didn't know how to communicate with the other 300 students. They didn't know sign language. Ida worried if they would accept her. They did.

She couldn't hear the band play or the cheerleaders cheer. But if being deaf is a handicap, no one told Ida. She joined the girls' varsity basketball team and worked hard. Wearing a hearing aid that allows her to detect the vibrations from the referee's whistle, she became the school's top scorer and team leader. In her senior year Ida took Tombstone to the semifinals in the state playoffs.

The last lesson is the most important. Don't let your fears get in the way of your dreams. Don't let what you can't do interfere with what you can do.

*The greatest victory is the victory over ourselves. Remember, it's always too soon to quit.*

If you would like more information on *Mind Gym* programs or products, please send an e-mail to batmack@ aol.com or write to

Gary Mack@Mind Gym
4455 East Moonlight Drive
Paradise Valley, Arizona 85253